THE FLYGERIANS
COOKBOOK

THE FLYGERIANS
COOKBOOK

OVER 70 RECIPES FOR
NIGERIAN FOOD THAT WILL
SPEAK TO YOUR SOUL &
WARM YOUR HEART

JESS & JO EDUN

PHOTOGRAPHY BY CLARE WINFIELD

RYLAND PETERS & SMALL
LONDON • NEW YORK

*Dedicated to our incredible Grandma
'Mama' – Mary Uhunamure Obahiagbon
– who passed 22nd February 2011.
Without her there would be no Flygerians.
We want to honour her beautiful life
and the love she showered us with.*

*To our mother Gloria Shomope-Edun
and father Godspower Edun.*

Senior Designer Megan Smith
Senior Editor Abi Waters
Head of Production Patricia
    Harrington
Creative Director Leslie Harrington
Editorial Director Julia Charles
Indexer Vanessa Bird
Food stylist Kathy Kordalis
Props stylist Max Robinson

First published in 2024 by
Ryland Peters & Small
20–21 Jockey's Fields, London
WC1R 4BW
and
341 E 116th St, New York NY 10029
www.rylandpeters.com

10 9 8 7 6 5 4 3 2 1

Text copyright © Jess Edun and
Jo Edun 2024
Design and commisioned
photography copyright © Ryland
Peters & Small 2024

ISBN: 978-1-78879-622-4

Printed in China

A CIP record for this book is
available from the British Library.

US Library of Congress Cataloging-
in-Publication Data has been
applied for.

NOTES
• Both British (metric) and
American (imperial plus US cups)
measurements are included in
these recipes for your convenience,
however, it is important to work
with one set of measurements
and not alternate between the
two within a recipe.
• All spoon measurements are
level unless otherwise specified.
• All eggs are medium (UK) or large
(US), unless specified as large, in
which case US extra-large should be
used. Uncooked or partially cooked
eggs should not be served to the
very old, frail, young children,
pregnant women or those with
compromised immune systems.
• Ovens should be preheated
to the specified temperatures.
We recommend using an oven
thermometer. If using a fan-assisted
oven, adjust temperatures according
to the manufacturer's instructions.
• When a recipe calls for the grated
zest of citrus fruit, buy unwaxed
fruit and wash well before using.
If you can only find treated fruit,
scrub well in warm soapy water
before using.

FSC
MIX
Paper from
responsible sources
FSC® C106563
www.fsc.org

CONTENTS

INTRODUCTION 6

NIGERIAN FOOD CULTURE 10

THE NIGERIAN KITCHEN 14

BASIC RECIPES 18

1 SMALL CHOPS 24

2 BIG CHOPS 50

3 SWALLOW & SIDES 86

4 STREET FOOD 94

5 SWEET THINGS 118

6 DRINKS 144

INDEX 174

ACKNOWLEDGEMENTS 176

CHOP LIFE BEFORE LIFE CHOPS YOU!

No wo(man) is an island. To know where you're going, you need to know where you have been. Our story is not only our own, but the beautiful journey of all the women before us who have paved the way for us to become the dual-nationality, Nigerian display of excellence, joy and warmth we are today.

We dedicate this book to our grandma Mary and our mother Gloria Shomope-Edun and father Godspower Edun who all taught us not only to demand a seat at the table, but to create our own.

Our journey is intertwined with those of our siblings, who taught us to love unapologetically, to be our true authentic selves, to be the light in times of darkness and to fight for what we believe in. What we believe in is spreading joy and creating a community that serves those who we have the pleasure of being around and cooking for. We did not get here alone and have the brilliant minds within our team to thank, who share our vision of sharing the love for our culture through our love of cooking, and bringing an energetic, unforgettable vibe that we stand before you to share today.

We are The Flygerians, two larger than life sisters, best friends and Nigerian restaurant owners. The Flygerians is more than just our name. It's a term used to describe a cool, ambitious, driven, forward-thinking Nigerian and it captivates our passion to be the best, shatter boundaries and put no limitation on the level we can reach.

Expect authentic recipes passed down through generations and new street food creations with a Flygerian twist.

We are bringing the sweet taste of Nigeria to not just the UK but the world. Our beautiful, tastebud-tantalizing Nigerian culture is too rich and vibrant not to share. Within the pages of this book, be prepared to be transported to Nigeria without ever needing to board a plane. We learned to cook from the ages of nine and ten in our grandma's kitchen in Hackney, East London. She would host community cookouts and invite every Tom, Dami and Harry from the block and sometimes even the random woman walking past with her dog who happened to smell the sweet scent of puff puff in the air!

We are two of eight siblings and as children our parents would leave all of us with our grandma (Mama) over the summer holidays, along with six cousins. Days and weeks would pass, as we spent our days cooking, laughing and snuggled under blankets in the living room swapping stories with our cousins way past our bed time. We remember waking up at 4 o'clock in the morning (while our cousins still slept) climbing out of bed and running to bathe, to ensure our Mama would take us with her to meet the early morning traders in Dalston market to get the best produce. Even with sleep still in our eyes, we could think of nothing better than helping our Mama carry the ingredients home

THE FLYGERIANS

NIGERIAN STREET FOOD

ready to cook one of her sensational soul-enriching meals. Little did we know at the time, that those days and weeks spent with our Mama and cousins, those moments we treasured forever, would shape not only our lives but eventually our careers as chefs. We would spend hours in the kitchen with our Mama back then, turning the bowl and washing the dishes, all the while learning her recipes inside out and how to cook and season them to perfection until we heard our ancestors whisper, 'That's enough my child...'. We would dance round the kitchen with Mama to Fela Kuti and listen to her stories of her own childhood, while she handed us small tasters of the hot akara she had just made, asking for our expert opinions on how it tasted.

Our Mama meant the world to us, and our incredible mother and father made sure we practised the dishes we had learned each summer at home with our siblings and at Christmas when all the family came over to our home. Most importantly our grandma also taught us that good food should hold no boundaries and should be enjoyed by all. Social inclusion was what our Mama lived by, and this was passed onto our mother and onto us. We believe no matter your race, gender, religion or sexual orientation, you should be invited into a space where you can feel safe to be yourself and enjoy yourself, a space where you can leave your troubles at the door and feel welcome. We live by this ethos and social inclusion is one of the fundamental values echoed throughout our business.

We both come from very education-driven backgrounds; Jess has a law degree and Jo is a fully qualified occupational therapist. As much as we both smashed our chosen professions, we always

knew we also wanted to make a real difference in another way and make our own mark in this world. When our beloved Mama Mary passed in 2011 we vowed that her legacy would live on within us and that her food, and our own spin-off recipes that she inspired, would open doors we could only have dared dream of. Our first-ever Flygerians restaurant opened in Peckham (dubbed the mini-Lagos of the UK) and this book embodies all that is wonderful about both our business and our South London home. Through running the restaurant and now writing this book we plan to make The Flygerians a household name globally, but all the while making sure that this book truly represents the community that we grew up in.

We invite you to enjoy the beautiful pages that follow and take inspiration from them, whether you are hosting dinners for family, friends and loved ones or simply making a meal for one to warm your soul. We want to make you feel like you belong, whether you are missing home or want to feel a part of our ever-growing Flygerians community. And remember, no one gets left behind, in our restaurant and in our book, so we have included something for everyone here. Meat-eaters, you know the vibe – we got you! Vegan? Oya come and chop! Pescatarian? We beg you, pull up a chair immediately!

We hope that our recipes and stories will bring you comfort and joy and help you to celebrate being a part of our epic Nigerian culture, as we always have and always will.

Jess & Jo xxx

NIGERIAN FOOD CULTURE

Despite there being hundreds of tribes and different religions within Nigeria, there is one thing that is distinctive across the country – our big, bold, charismatic and gassed-up personalities. You will know you have encountered a Nigerian without them even mentioning where they are from. This is what our slogan is based upon, 'Chop life before life chops you', which means you must enjoy life before it's too late. No matter what you are doing in life, make sure you have fun and enjoy yourself. We chop life through cooking food that brings everyone together.

There is no exact number within the country, but some have counted around 500 different tribes. The top four most common and widely known ones are:

EDO (BENIN'S) This is the tribe that our grandmother is from. It is located in the southern region of the country. Our recipes and cooking methods are derived mainly from the Edo style of cooking, mixed with a little British cooking style too. Ogbono soup is a popular dish eaten by the Edo people. Ogbono seeds originate from African wild mango, also known as 'bush mango'. These seeds are then dried and blended to give the soup a 'draw effect' (that delicious pull you get when you scoop up the stew).

YORUBA Our grandfather was from the Yoruba tribe, and our parents spent a lot of their youth at school and living in Lagos. Ayamase is a popular Yoruban stew, also known as 'designer stew' as it is usually cooked on special occasions with rich ingredients. This is one for the heat lovers – stay clear if you suffer from heartburn or gastric reflux as you might be in for a rough night, haha! Ayamase is heavily oil based and made from a lot of green scotch bonnets and green bell peppers. For what it lacks in appearance it makes up for in taste. This recipe traditionally uses quite a complex method but we have tweaked it to use ofada oil, which is bleached (burnt) palm oil, giving the ayamase its dark colour and smoky flavour.

HAUSA-FULANI This tribe is located in the north of the country and is the biggest Muslim tribe in Nigeria. The tribe is most famously known as the creators of suya spice and the finest grilled meat.

IGBO (also spelled Ibo) This tribe is also located in southern Nigeria and best known as the major farmers of cassava and yam. We love to eat goat meat pepper soup with boiled yam, which is a popular dish among the Igbo tribe.

CHOP & GO

Certainly! Nigerian cuisine offers a diverse array of snacks and meals, ranging from savoury to sweet, which often reflects the country's rich culinary heritage. Here's a list of some popular Nigerian food for you to discover and enjoy:

CHIN CHIN Nigeria's answer to a biscuit/cookie (see page 128). It's a crunchy, deep-fried snack made from a dough of flour, sugar, butter, milk and sometimes eggs. It can be flavoured with spices like nutmeg, coconut, Biscoff and/or vanilla and is often cut into small rectangles or diamond shapes before frying.

PUFF PUFF A sweet and fluffy fried dough ball, similar to a doughnut/donut, made from a simple batter of flour, sugar, yeast and water. It can be flavoured with any topping you like. Once you have mastered the basic recipe (see page 127) it can be flavoured with Oreos, cinnamon and stuffed with jam or chocolate.

SUYA One of the most famous and popular Nigerian street-food snacks (see page 36). When in Nigeria you must try the 'University of Suya' restaurant located in Lagos. We applaud them as their suya is sensational. Suya is the peanut-based spice that accompanies the grilled meat, which are then presented on skewers or wrapped in newspaper.

AKARA A deep-fried bean cake made from blended black-eyed peas mixed with onions, peppers and spices, shaped into balls or patties and deep-fried until golden brown (see page 29).

MEAT PIE Nigerian meat pies are savoury pastries filled with a mixture of seasoned minced/ground meat (often beef or chicken), onions and vegetables such as carrots and peas (see page 108). The filling is encased in a flaky pastry dough and baked until golden brown. The filling can be swapped for vegetarian/vegan filling if preferred.

PLANTAIN CHIPS Thinly sliced plantains that are deep-fried until crispy. They can be seasoned with salt, pepper or spices for extra flavour and are enjoyed like a packet of crisps/chips (see page 103).

CHAPMAN A welcome drink made from Nigerian fanta and sprite, then spiced up with fresh fruit and aromatic bitters (see page 146). It is typically served as a mocktail but we enjoy it with a double shot of naughty Uncle Wray rum, Hennessy or vodka.

ZOBO A thicker and richer welcome drink made from hibiscus flower (see page 154). Caribbeans also refer to this drink as sorrel.

SOUPS & STEWS Soups and stews are central to Nigerian cuisine. They are usually thick and hearty, often served with a staple such as rice, pounded yam, fufu (a starchy dough made from cassava, yams, or plantains), or eba (garri, a fermented cassava product). Popular soups and stews include Egusi Soup (see page 59), Ogbono Soup (see page 60) and Banga Soup (see page 63). Popular stews are Ayamase (see page 70), Oxtail Stew (see page 68) and Efo Riro (see page 71).

NIGERIAN COOKING METHODS

There are some common cooking methods and ingredients used in Nigerian cooking.

GRILLING & ROASTING These are common cooking methods for meats and fish. Grilled or roasted meats are often seasoned with a variety of spices and served with side dishes or eaten as snacks. Suya is a popular dish that is usually grilled.

FRYING Another popular cooking method in Nigerian cuisine. Fried foods include items like plantains (dodo), bean cakes (akara) and Puff Puff (deep-fried dough balls).

AIR-FRYING This cooking method is rapidly taking over the cooking industry, with everyone looking for different ways to eat cleaner and healthier. If you're feeling bold and daring, try this method for making meat pies, suya, fried fish and our Lekki Express Shawarma (see page 99).

STEAMING & BOILING Steaming and boiling are used to cook a variety of dishes, including rice, moi moi, beans, eggs, vegetables and certain types of soups and stews.

TRADITIONAL COOKING TECHNIQUES Traditional cooking techniques such as pounding, grinding, and fermenting are also used in Nigerian cuisine to prepare certain dishes and ingredients.

BAKING This is not a common method used in Nigeria but it is a growing cooking technique as people are looking for healthier methods of cooking dishes rather than frying.

Overall, Nigerian cooking involves a combination of all these methods and ingredients (see pages 15–17), resulting in flavourful and diverse dishes that reflect the country's rich culinary heritage. We have added a few boujee cooking techniques along the way – we are soft-life babes that don't always want to break our nails or arms endlessly pounding ingredients. Check out our pounded yam recipe (see page 88), which we make in a food processor rather than the traditional way.

ENTERTAINING THE NIGERIAN WAY

There are a few funny cultural mannerisms that you should know about before hosting a fellow Nigerian.

» If you invite us to your house, we expect to be fed.

» Serve food with your right hand and not your left hand (your left hand is perceived as your dirty hand), although this is more for the elders.

» When serving food, ensure you also serve a drink.

» When serving swallow food (see pages 88–92), provide a bowl of warm water and lemon before and after a meal to allow guests to wash their hands.

» Always cook more than you think you need – you can never have too much food, and we like to leave with leftovers.

» Nigerian culture is about bringing people together, so if you are celebrating an event, expect extra guests – we love to celebrate life together.

» When hosting an event, don't expect your guests to arrive on time – if the party starts at 6pm, your Nigerian guests will arrive at 8pm if you're lucky.

» Leave salt and pepper on the table, and some chilli/chili oil, because everyone's taste and desired heat level is different.

Nigerian hospitality is all about abundance and respect. Anyone that enters our home is treated with generosity and warmth. Our guests are our family and whatever we do, no matter how big or small, we love to share, as we love life and the people who chose to embrace in our culture.

THE NIGERIAN KITCHEN

One thing about Nigerians is that we are always going to have food in abundance in our houses, and we will be ready for our guests when you pop by to say hello. There will always be a big batch of stew or jollof in the fridge in Tupperware that used to hold a family sized amount of ice cream. And if there isn't anything left from our big batch cooking, then we will whip something up.

FRESH INGREDIENTS

Our beloved Mama was originally from Benin City and migrated to Lagos, the capital of Nigeria, in the early 1960s. Our grandma had all these ingredients to hand in her kitchen growing up in Nigeria, but for us, growing up in the 1990s in the UK, these ingredients could only be found in Dalston or Peckham markets. Now we have the luxury of ordering them online or from our local supermarket. Influenced by various cultures and regions within the country, here are some fresh ingredients commonly found in a Nigerian kitchen:

LEAFY GREENS Various leafy greens such as spinach, ugwu (fluted pumpkin leaves), bitter leaf (see below) and waterleaf are used in Nigerian cooking, adding nutrients and flavour to dishes.

FRESH BITTER LEAVES These are exactly what they suggest – bitter leaves. Its botanical name is Vernonia amygdalina and is a popular vegetable used across West Africa and typically added to Ogbono and Egusi recipes.

OKRA Okra is a popular vegetable in Nigeria, used in dishes like Seafood Okra soup (see page 56).

YAMS, CASSAVA & PLANTAINS These starchy staples are commonly used in Nigerian cuisine, boiled, fried or pounded to make swallow food.

PEPPERS Peppers are a staple in Nigerian cuisine, including bell peppers, habanero peppers (known as ata-rodo) and Scotch bonnet peppers. They add heat and flavour to many dishes.

TOMATOES Nigeria is the second largest producer of tomatoes in Africa and the twelfth largest globally. This is a must-have fresh ingredient for us, but canned works just as well because of its long-life durability. Tomatoes are used in many Nigerian dishes, either fresh or in purée/paste form as a base for stews and sauces.

ONIONS (WHITE OR RED) Onions are a fundamental ingredient in Nigerian cooking, used for flavouring stews, soups and sauces.

CHICKEN Chicken is widely consumed in Nigeria. Typically, Nigerians use 'broiler chicken' for soups and stews as it is tougher in texture and good for cooking stews as the meat does not easily fall off the bone. However, we have not used 'broiler chicken' within our recipes as we prefer our meat to be tender. Use whatever chicken you prefer.

FISH Fish is a staple protein source in Nigeria, particularly in coastal regions. Various types of fish are used including tilapia, catfish and snapper.

ASSORTED MEATS (OFFAL) Nigerian cuisine often includes assorted meats, also known as offal, which includes parts such as liver, kidney, tripe (shaki), cow skin (pomo) and cow foot.

PANTRY

Nigerian cuisine often includes a variety of dried ingredients from the storecupboard, such as grains (rice, maize, millet), pulses/legumes (beans, lentils), spices and herbs. Here are a few of our favourites that we keep well stocked in:

GOLDEN SELLA BASMATI RICE This is a type of parboiled rice that is usually sold in larger quantities and perfect for when you are cooking for a crowd. Easy cook long grain or basmati rice is a good alternative.

YAJI (SUYA SPICE) A blend of groundnut powder, pepper and other spices used to season meats, particularly for making suya (see page 36), a popular Nigerian street food.

AFRICAN DRIED CHILLI PEPPER Also known as 'African bird's eye chillies'. Dried under the sun, these are hotter than the average chilli, so always use with caution.

DRIED/GROUND CRAYFISH Crayfish are freshwater crustaceans resembling small lobsters. In Nigeria they are cleaned and dried under the sun and smoked to preserve. Can be used whole or ground.

DRIED STOCKFISH (PALNA) Stockfish is made from dried and salted cod or other white fish, dried and sometimes salted. It is perfect for making soups and stews as it is not too brittle in texture.

GARLIC When we say these are essential, we mean that when you are down to your last 4 garlic bulbs, run and buy more immediately. Garlic is an essential ingredient used for flavouring many Nigerian dishes. Slow cooked, it adds an extra sweetness.

GINGER Ginger is used both for its flavour and its medicinal properties in Nigerian cuisine. It's commonly used in stews, soups and immune-boosting health drinks as on page 164.

FRESH HERBS Herbs such as African basil (scent leaf), mint, parsley and coriander/cilantro are used to add freshness and aroma to dishes.

MEAT & FISH

BEEF One of the most common meats used in Nigerian cuisine. It is used in various dishes such as stews, soups and grilled or fried dishes. It tastes sensational when used to suya (see page 36).

GOAT Goat meat is popular in Nigerian cuisine and is often used in stews, soups and grilled dishes.

LOCUST BEANS (IRU) Beans from the locust bean tree, also known as *Parkia biglobosa*, which is a native tree to West Africa. The beans are typically fermented over several weeks to allow the pungent aroma. We use iru in our Vegan Efo Riro recipe on page 71.

GARRI A flour made from cassava. Mixed with water and palm oil (Edo style) it makes the swallow dish, Eba (see page 91).

NIGERIAN GUINNESS Brewed in Nigeria and known for its high alcohol content. It is thicker in body and sweeter in taste than Irish Guinness.

SEEDS There are a variety of popular seeds that are used across Nigeria to thicken different soups and stews including ogbono seeds from the African bush mango and egusi seeds from melons. To prepare they are typically blended to a course texture and stirred into a delicious soup.

PALM OIL Palm oil is a cooking oil used in Nigerian cuisine, particularly in the preparation of soups and stews. It adds a distinct flavour and colour to dishes. When purchasing palm oil, it is best to check if it has been certified sustainable by Roundtable on Sustainable Palm Oil (RSPO) to ensure it was ethically produced.

PALM NUT EXTRACT Derived from the seed found inside the fruit of the palm tree.

And not forgetting these other pantry essentials that we always make sure we are well stocked in:

» Jumbo stock powder (chicken, fish, beef)
» Bouillon vegetable stock powder
» Cornflour/cornstarch
» Dried thyme
» Dried mixed herbs
» Bay leaves (fresh and dried)
» Paprika
» Garlic powder
» Curry powder (mild, medium or hot)
» Ofada oil (bleached palm oil)
» Vegetable oil
» Palm wine

CHILLI H'OIL

After church, we eat Chinese food. This recipe is paying homage to all the Chinese restaurants typically packed out on Sunday afternoons with the congregation waiting to be fed.

250 g/9 oz. dried whole chillies/ chiles
100 g/3½ oz. dried crayfish
1 teaspoon black peppercorns
2 calabash nutmegs
3 spring onions/scallions, minced
2-cm/1-inch piece of fresh ginger, minced
4 garlic cloves, minced
500 ml/2 cups peanut oil (or vegetable oil)
2 teaspoons sesame seeds
1 tablespoon honey
1 tablespoon salt or Jumbo chicken stock powder (or to taste)

MAKES 2 X 500-ML/18-OZ. JARS

BLEND IT
Using a spice grinder or blender, add the whole chillies, crayfish and black peppercorns and grind to a coarse powder.

Grind the calabash nutmeg separately and sift as the shell is not edible.

In a food processor, mince the spring onions, ginger and garlic.

HEAT IT UP
In a small pot, heat the oil over a medium heat, infuse the dried and processed ingredients and stir well.

Add the sesame seeds, honey and salt to the pot, stir well and cook over a low heat for 5 minutes. Leave the Chilli H'oil to cool.

CHOP
Serve with anything and store in a jar in a cool place or fridge for up to 3 months.

GHANAIAN SHITO

Shito is a beautiful chilli/chile sauce of joy that we discovered from our Ghanaian neighbours. This is an absolute banger that sends us to the depths of the earth our feet are yet to reach. This is to honour our beautiful brothers and sisters of Ghana, whose culture, just like ours, is rich in history of kings and queens and echoes a beautiful ancestry of excellence and an abundance of prosperity before anything else. We hope our version of this beautiful sauce does you justice. Also known as 'Black Chilli Oil', this is a spicy condiment made from chillies, onions, spices and fish or prawns/shrimp.

500 g/1 lb. 2 oz. dried chillies/ chiles (such as African bird's eye chilli or Scotch bonnet)

2 large onions, chopped

1 large garlic, crushed/minced

1 tablespoon grated fresh ginger

150 g/5½ oz. dried prawn/ shrimp or fish flakes (optional)

2 tablespoons dried crayfish (for maximum flavour) (optional)

220 ml/scant 1 cup vegetable oil

2 tablespoons ground black pepper

1 tablespoon ground cloves

1 teaspoon ground coriander

1 teaspoon ground nutmeg

1 teaspoon salt, or to taste

1 tablespoon Jumbo prawn/ shrimp or fish stock powder

120g/⅓ cup tomato purée/paste

blender/ food processor

SERVES 2-20

(DEPENDING ON WHAT YOU ARE USING IT FOR – SLOWLY OVER TIME OR AT A DINNER PARTY FOR LARGE GROUPS)

BEGIN BY PREPARING THE DRIED CHILLI PEPPERS

Remove the stems and seeds from the chillies, then soak them in hot water for about 30 minutes to soften.

Drain the soaked chillies and place them in a blender or food processor along with the onions, garlic, ginger, dried prawn or fish flakes and dried crayfish, if using. Blend until you have a smooth paste, adding a little water if needed to help the blending process.

HEAT THE OIL

Heat the vegetable oil in a large saucepan or Dutch oven over a medium heat. Add the blended chilli mixture to the hot oil and stir well to combine. Cook the mixture, stirring occasionally, for 15–20 minutes, or until it reduces and thickens slightly.

Add the black pepper, ground cloves, coriander and nutmeg, salt, stock powder and tomato purée to the pot. Stir well to combine.

Reduce the heat to low and simmer the shito sauce for another 30–40 minutes, stirring occasionally, or until it thickens to your desired consistency and the flavours meld together.

TASTE TEST

Taste the shito sauce and adjust the seasoning as needed, adding more salt or spices if desired.

Leave to cool completely before transferring to clean, airtight jars or containers for storage. Store the shito sauce in the refrigerator for up to several weeks. It will develop more flavour over time.

AGEGE BREAD

Ag-e-ge bread is a sweet Nigerian bread that is chopped 24/7.

70 g/⅓ cup granulated sugar
250 ml/1 cup warm water
    (about 45°C/110°F)
10 g/⅓ oz. instant yeast
500 g/3½ cups bread flour
    (plain/all-purpose flour can
    be used as a substitute),
    plus extra for dusting
1 teaspoon salt
50 g/3½ tablespoons unsalted
    butter, at room temperature
vegetable oil or butter,
    for greasing

2 x medium loaf pans

MAKES 2 LOAVES

GRAB A BOWL

Mix the sugar and warm water together in a small bowl. Mix until the sugar is fully dissolved. Sprinkle the yeast over the water, leave it for 5–10 minutes, or until it begins to foam. This suggests that the yeast is active.

In a large mixing bowl, combine the bread flour and salt. Make a well in the centre and pour in the yeast mixture. Add the softened butter. Using a wooden spoon or your hands, mix until a rough dough forms.

LET'S GET PHYSICAL

Transfer the dough to a floured surface and knead it for about 10–15 minutes until it becomes smooth and elastic. You may need to add a little extra flour if the dough is too sticky.

Clean and grease a large mixing bowl with vegetable oil. Place the dough into the bowl, spin it to coat with oil. Cover the bowl with clean cling film/plastic wrap and let it rise in a warm place for about 1–2 hours, or until it doubles in size.

Once the dough has risen, punch it down to deflate it and transfer it to a lightly floured surface. Using a rolling pin, roll out the dough and fold it into itself.

BAKE TIME

Divide the dough in half and place into the greased loaf pans. Lightly cover the dough with cling film and leave to rise for 40 minutes.

Preheat the oven to 180°C/350°F/Gas 4.

The dough should have doubled in size, gently brush the tops with a little water. This helps create a softer crust. Bake the loaves in the preheated oven for 25–30 minutes, or until they are golden brown.

Remove the bread from oven and set aside to cool.

TIME TO CHOP!

1

SMALL CHOPS

MOI MOI
STEAMED BEAN PUDDING

Moi Moi is a steamed bean pudding made from blended and skinless
black-eyed beans. It can be cooked vegan style or plumped up with meat,
fish or crustacean options and can be served as an appetizer.

500 g/3 cups peeled and dried
black-eyed beans

1 large onion, chopped

3 red Romano peppers

3 red Scotch bonnet chilli/chile
(or to taste)

4 garlic cloves

60 g/2 oz. Jumbo chicken stock
powder or bouillon vegetable
stock powder

20 g/¾ oz. ground crayfish
(optional)

2 tablespoons dried mixed herbs

2 tablespoons curry powder
(mild, medium or hot)

100 ml/⅓ cup vegetable oil

2 UK medium/US large eggs,
beaten (optional)

Moi Moi leaves, rinsed, or foil
containers

100 ml/⅓ cup boiling water

salt

OPTIONAL FILLINGS

6 hard-boiled eggs, peeled
and halved

200 g/7 oz. raw tiger prawns/
shrimp

4 x 100-g/3½-oz. cans of
mackerel, fish shredded

MAKES 10–12 PUDDINGS

FIRST, PREPARE THE BEANS

Soak the peeled black-eyed beans in boiling water for 30 minutes. Using
a sieve, rinse and drain the beans to ensure there is no excess skin.

Blend the soaked beans, onion, Romano peppers, Scotch bonnet
chillies and garlic in a food processor until you achieve a smooth
consistency. Add water to assist with the blend if necessary.

Transfer the blended mixture to a bowl and add all the stock powder,
ground crayfish, if using, mixed herbs, curry powder, a pinch of salt,
vegetable oil and beaten eggs, if using.

FORMATION

Rinse the Moi Moi leaves, if using this method, and prepare them to
fold into parcels. Baste each Moi Moi leaf with oil to avoid the leaves
becoming dry or sticking (or baste the foil containers if using).

If you are adding the optional fillings, half fill the parcel (or container)
with the bean mixture. Add the sliced eggs or raw prawns and mackerel
and top with some more bean mixture, then wrap the leaves over the
top to make a parcel, or top with the container lid.

START STEAMING

Place the filled Moi Moi puddings in the base of a medium saucepan
and add the boiling water. Steam for 50 minutes over a medium heat,
using a probe or toothpick to check the consistency. Add more water
to the pan as needed to prevent burning. Leave to cool before serving.

CHOP LIFE!

TIPS

» To ensure you don't overheat your blender, add ingredients in
batches and add small amounts of water to aid smooth blending.

» Adding raw eggs to the mixture gives the Moi Moi a soft and fluffy
finish. If you don't use eggs, you can add additional oil instead.

» If you are worried about the tightness of your parcels, you can use
twine to secure them if needed.

VEGAN AKARA BEAN FRITTERS

Akara is a vegan Nigerian snack, which is the perfect small chop to have while you wait for your main course. Originally vegan and gluten free, it is a dish for everyone. Akara can be served hot as a small chop, but is also delicious with shop-bought Nigerian (or Madagascan to honour our dual nationality) custard for breakfast.

500 g/3 cups peeled black-eyed beans
1 Scotch bonnet chilli/chile (or more for preference)
1 red Romano pepper
2 garlic cloves (optional)
1 large red onion, chopped
1 tablespoon bouillon vegetable stock powder
1 teaspoon baking powder
1 tablespoon dried mixed herbs
salt
vegetable oil, for deep frying

MAKES 15-20 AKARAS

FIRST, PREPARE THE BEANS
Submerge the black-eyed peas in boiling water and soak for 1 hour. They will get softer as a result, making blending easier.

Once the black-eyed peas are soaked, drain the water, and transfer them to a blender or food processor. Add the Scotch bonnet, Romano pepper, garlic and red onion and blend to a smooth paste. Try to make the mixture as thick as you can, but you might need to add a little water to aid blending. Also try blending in stages to avoid the blender overheating.

Pour the blended mixture into a large bowl. Stir thoroughly and add the vegetable stock powder, baking powder, mixed herbs and salt to taste.

START FRYING
Heat the vegetable oil in a deep frying pan/skillet over a medium heat to about 180°C/350°F. To test if the oil is ready for frying if you don't have a thermometer, drop a small piece of bread into the pan. If it sizzles and browns straight away, it's ready; if not heat for a little longer.

You can shape the fritter mixture into balls or flatten them slightly into patties, depending on your preference, or just use a deep spoon to scoop up some of the bean mixture and carefully drop it into the heated oil. Be cautious of splattering as they enter the pan.

Fry the akara until golden brown and crispy, turning occasionally to ensure even cooking. This should take about 5 minutes per batch.

LET'S CHOP!
Once cooked, place the akara on paper towels to drain excess oil and repeat this process until the mixture has all been used.

EWA AGOYIN

This is a traditional Nigerian dish made from black-eyed beans, and can be made vegan by swapping or taking out ingredients. In our opinion it can be eaten any time of the day but then again we don't believe in placing restrictions on food. Ewa Agoyin can be served with boiled yam or cassava, Agege bread (see page 23), or fried plantains. If you are feeling extra, you can add a fried egg on top.

500 g/3 cups black-eyed peas or brown beans
salt and freshly ground black pepper
2–4 fried eggs, to serve (optional)

AGOYIN SAUCE
2 large red onions, chopped
6 garlic cloves
5 Scotch bonnet chillies/chiles (or to taste)
10 cherry tomatoes
1 red Romano pepper
150 ml/⅔ cup palm oil or olive oil
2 tablespoons Jumbo prawn/ shrimp stock powder or bouillon vegetable stock powder
1 tablespoon paprika
3 teaspoons ground crayfish (optional)
2 tablespoons curry powder (mild, medium or hot)
salt

SERVES 2-4 FLY PEOPLE

FIRST, PREPARE THE BEANS

Place the black-eyed beans in a colander and rinse thoroughly.

Put the beans in a large pot with a pinch of salt and add boiling water to cover. Boil the beans for 1½ hours until tender, topping up with more water as needed. Drain, then return the beans to the pot and roughly mash.

MAKE THE AGOYIN SAUCE

Using a food processor, blend the red onions, garlic cloves, Scotch bonnets, cherry tomatoes and Romano pepper.

In a deep saucepan, heat the oil and add the blended onion mixture. Season with the stock powder, paprika, ground crayfish, if using, and curry powder.

Take the sauce off the heat once it has thickened and the flavours have combined. Check the seasoning and add salt to taste.

LET'S CHOP!

To serve, transfer a portion of the cooked beans to a dish or plate and drizzle a lot of Agoyin sauce over the top. Top with a fried egg, if liked, and season with freshly ground black pepper.

GIZDODO SKEWERS

Gizdodo gets its name from gizzards and *dodo* (plantain) being mixed. Chicken and turkey gizzard is a popular small chop eaten in Nigeria. Our grandma used to make us these skewers as a snack to graze on.

500 g/1 lb. 2 oz. chicken gizzards

1 tablespoon ground ginger

1 tablespoon Jumbo chicken stock powder

1 tablespoon dried thyme

2 tablespoons curry powder (mild, medium or hot)

2 tablespoons ground turmeric

2 tablespoons garlic powder

2 bell peppers (any colour), deseeded and cut into large pieces

2 large red onions, cut into large pieces

1 large white onion, peeled and roughly chopped

5 red Romano peppers, roughly chopped

2 red Scotch bonnet chillies/chiles (or more to taste)

3–4 garlic cloves

150 ml/⅔ cup vegetable oil, plus extra for shallow frying

2 ripe plantains, peeled and sliced into thick rounds

400 g/1 cup tomato purée/paste

salt

15 wooden skewers (no need to presoak)

SERVES 3–4 FLY PEOPLE

FIRST, PREPARE THE GIZZARDS

Add the gizzards to a large saucepan and add the ginger, chicken stock powder, dried thyme, curry powder, turmeric, garlic powder and a pinch of salt. Pour sufficient boiling water into the pot to submerge the meat and cook over a medium heat for 30–40 minutes until tender. Top up the water if it begins to evaporate.

GET BAKING

Preheat the oven to 200°C/400°F/Gas 6. Place the peppers and red onions on a baking sheet, season with salt and roast for 15–20 minutes.

PROCESS & FRY

Using a food processor, blitz the chopped white onion, Romano peppers, Scotch bonnets and garlic together until minced.

In a deep frying pan/skillet, shallow fry the plantain slices in vegetable oil until golden brown. (As the plantain is quite ripe it may appear to be burning but this is OK.) Remove the plantain from the pan and set aside until needed.

Drain the cooked gizzards and set the stock water aside.

Using the same pan, fry the gizzards in vegetable oil for 3–4 minutes.

ADD THE FLAVOUR

In a separate pan, add the vegetable oil, tomato purée and the blended white onion mixture and fry for 2–3 minutes.

Add 250 ml/1 cup reserved gizzard stock water, stir until the mixture has combined, then cook for 5 minutes over a low heat. Leave the lid off the pot to allow the water to reduce and add seasoning to taste.

Turn the heat off and add the fried plantain and gizzards to the pan allowing the cooked sauce to evenly coat all the ingredients. Stir gently to avoid the plantain slices from breaking up.

BRING IT ALL TOGETHER

Thread the pepper, onion, plantain and gizzard onto the skewers, continuing until all the ingredients have been used.

LET'S CHOP!

BEEF SUYA

This is Nigeria's number one street food, with its melt-in-the-mouth texture, bursting with cultural history and, most importantly, vibes. To be chopped in abundance with the masses, beef suya is the perfect snack or main showstopper for every occasion, with its unique barbecue, like no other, beautiful flavours. It's perfect to be made on a barbecue or on a grill/broiler pan.

850 g/1 lb. 14 oz. sirloin steak,
   thinly sliced
4 tablespoons vegetable oil
2 teaspoons salt
1 large onion, diced
3 large tomatoes, diced
chopped fresh parsley,
   to garnish (optional)

MARINADE
150 g/generous 1 cup roasted
   peanuts
2 tablespoons paprika
2 tablespoons onion powder
2 tablespoons ground ginger
4 tablespoons ground Scotch
   bonnet pepper (or to taste)
2 tablespoons garlic powder
1 tablespoon vegetable oil
2 calabash nutmeg, crushed
freshly ground black pepper

*10 metal or wooden skewers
   (soaked if wooden)*

SERVES 2-4 FLY PEOPLE

FIRST, MAKE THE MARINADE
Place the peanuts in a food processor and process until finely chopped. Add the paprika, onion powder, ginger, Scotch bonnet pepper, garlic powder and 1 tablespoon of the vegetable oil and pulse until combined.

Separately blend the calabash nutmeg with a pinch of black pepper. Sift this into the peanut mixture and mix together.

SOAK UP THE FLAVOUR
Place the sliced steak in a large bowl or shallow dish. Drizzle with the vegetable oil, sprinkle with the salt and toss to coat. Add the peanut mixture and toss again to coat. Refrigerate, covered, for 2 hours.

WEAVE IT
Drain the beef, discarding the marinade, then thread the meat onto the skewers.

GRILL TIME
Grill the beef, covered, turning occasionally, over a medium-high heat for 10–15 minutes, or until it reaches your desired doneness.

Serve with the diced onions, tomatoes and parsley, if using, as a garnish and watch the colour pop.

MIGHTY SUPERMALT WINGS

There is nothing like a Supermalt – this malty non-alcoholic sensational drink has earned its rightful place in the high ranks of all great Nigerian households. Its combined sweetness and maltiness is the reason for it cementing its firm place at every Nigerian social gathering. Nigerian culture is so diverse and when we cater, we seek to cater to all, so this showstopper dish is bound to have everybody from all walks of life wanting more. These wings were inspired by our Mama (Grandma), as Supermalt was one of her favourite drinks – we would dance around the kitchen from the age of nine until well into our early 20s, cooking up a storm and always drinking Supermalt.

1.5 kg/3¼ lb. chicken wings, split at the joint (no chewing tips round here, tips discarded please)
3 tablespoons olive oil
1 tablespoon Jumbo chicken stock powder
1 tablespoon salt
2 tablespoons freshly ground black pepper
3 teaspoons garlic powder
1 teaspoon onion powder
3 tablespoons smoked paprika
sesame seeds and chopped spring onions/scallions, to garnish (optional)

HONEY GLAZE
60 g/¼ cup organic honey
½ Scotch bonnet chilli/chile, finely chopped
120 g/½ cup Original Supermalt
2 garlic cloves, crushed/minced

SERVES 3-4 FLY PEOPLE

PREPARATION IS KEY
Preheat the oven to 200°C/400°F/Gas 6.

Toss the chicken wings with the olive oil, chicken stock powder, salt, black pepper, garlic powder, onion powder and smoked paprika, making sure the wings are evenly coated.

IT'S TIME TO GET THESE BAD BOYS COOKING
Arrange the wings on a baking sheet lined with foil, making sure they are not overcrowded.

Bake in the preheated oven for 45–50 minutes, or until the wings are golden brown and crispy all over, flipping them halfway through the cooking time.

MAKE THAT GLAZE
In a small saucepan over a medium heat, combine the honey, chopped Scotch bonnet, Supermalt and garlic. Bring the mixture to a simmer, stirring occasionally, and continue simmering for 5–7 minutes, or until the sauce thickens slightly – it should have a glossy shine to it.

Once the wings are done baking, put them in a large clean bowl. Pour the beautiful Supermalt glaze over the wings and toss them until evenly coated.

LET'S CHOP!
Who doesn't like a little aesthetic and cute presentation? Garnish with sesame seeds and spring onions, if liked, and serve the wings hot.

NOTE If you are not a fan of heat you can leave out the Scotch bonnet.

PRAWN CROQUETTES

Prawn croquettes are a delightful crispy small chop, which go down a treat
at dinner parties or events where guests are expecting a small snack.

2 tablespoons butter

4 garlic cloves, crushed/minced

4 large carrots, finely diced

1 small onion, finely chopped

500 g/1 lb. 2 oz. raw peeled
    and cleaned prawns/shrimp

1 Scotch bonnet chilli/chile
    (optional)

2 tablespoons chopped fresh
    parsley

1 tablespoon Jumbo prawn/
    shrimp stock powder

1 tablespoon dried thyme

1 tablespoon paprika

1 tablespoon mild curry powder

1 tablespoon dried chives

1 tablespoon dried mixed herbs

200 g/2 cups cornflour/
    cornstarch

250 ml/1 cup whole/full-fat milk
    (or soya milk)

4 spring onions/scallions,
    finely chopped

grated zest of 1 lemon

salt and freshly ground black
    pepper

FOR COATING & FRYING

500 g/5 cups cornflour/
    cornstarch

2 UK large/US extra-large eggs,
    beaten

vegetable oil for frying

MAKES 15-18 CROQUETTES

FIRST, MAKE THE FILLING

In a frying pan/skillet, melt the butter over a medium heat. Add the
garlic, carrots and onion and sauté for about 2–3 minutes until softened.

Using a food processor, mince the prawns, Scotch bonnet, if using, and
parsley to a coarse texture.

Add the minced prawn mixture to the frying pan, along with the prawn
stock powder, thyme, paprika, curry powder, dried chives and mixed
herbs, stirring frequently. Cook until the prawns turn pink.

BRING IT TOGETHER

Sprinkle the cornflour over the prawn mixture and stir well to combine.
Cook for a further 1–2 minutes to cook out the raw taste of the flour.

Gradually pour in the milk, while stirring continuously, to prevent lumps
from forming. Cook for about 2–3 minutes until the mixture thickens
and becomes creamy.

Season with salt to taste, then stir in the spring onions and lemon zest.
Remove from the heat and leave to cool.

GET SHAPING

Once the prawn filling has cooled, rub your hands with cornflour and
roll into bite-sized balls. Place the balls on a tray lined with baking
parchment and leave to rest in the fridge for 30 minutes.

Crack and whisk the eggs in a small bowl, adding a pinch of salt. Pour
the cornflour on a shallow plate. Dip each prawn croquette first into the
whisked eggs, then roll in the cornflour, making sure it's evenly coated.

LET'S FRY

Heat the vegetable oil in a deep frying pan to 180°C/350°F. To test if
the oil is ready for frying if you don't have a thermometer, drop a small
piece of bread into the pan. If it sizzles and browns straight away, it's
ready; if not heat for a little longer.

Once hot, gently add the croquettes and fry for about 3 minutes until
golden brown. Place on paper towels once fried to drain any excess oil.

Serve the prawn croquettes hot, either on their own or with our
homemade Chilli H'oil (see page 19) and mayonnaise.

BEEF SUYA
SPRING ROLLS

Suya spring rolls is what you get when two beautiful worlds collide. We are Nigerians who love pan-Asian food. Spring rolls was always a no-brainer as we love biting into the crispy crunch of the flaky pastry and revealing the filling inside. We decided to fuse this well-crafted, yet simple appetizer with Nigerian beef suya to create a party in your mouth with every bite.

500 g/2 cups cooked Suya Spiced Beef (see page 36)
1 onion, finely chopped
3 large (bell) peppers, finely chopped (red, green or yellow)
30 g/1 cup chopped fresh coriander/cilantro (optional)
35g/¼ cup chopped peanuts or cashews
2 tablespoons suya spice marinade (homemade, see page 36, or shop-bought)
500 ml/2 cups vegetable oil, for deep frying
salt and freshly ground black pepper

TO ASSEMBLE
10 spring roll wrappers (also known as spring roll pastry or lumpia wrappers)
200 ml/scant 1 cup water (for sealing the wrappers)
sweet chilli sauce or Chilli H'oil (see page 19), to serve (optional)

SERVES 2-4 FLY PEOPLE

START WITH SEASONING
In a large mixing bowl, combine the shredded suya beef with the onion, peppers, coriander, nuts and suya spice. Season with salt and pepper to taste. Mix well to ensure all the ingredients are evenly combined.

MAKE THE ROLLS
Lay out a spring roll wrapper on a clean, dry surface, with one corner pointing towards you (like a diamond shape). Place a spoonful of the suya filling near the bottom corner of the wrapper. Fold the bottom corner of the wrapper over the filling, tucking it snugly around the filling. Fold the left and right corners of the wrapper towards the centre. Moisten the top corner of the wrapper with water, then roll up the spring roll tightly towards the top corner, sealing the edges with the moistened corner.

Repeat the process 8 times with the remaining wrappers and filling. If there is any remaining filling, you can use the 2 remaining sheets. We like it meat rich, but you can spread it out slightly thinner.

GET FRYING
Heat the vegetable oil in a deep frying pan/skillet over a medium heat to 150–175°C/300–350°F. To test if the oil is ready for frying if you don't have a thermometer, drop a small piece of bread into the pan. If it sizzles and browns straight away, it's ready; if not heat for a little longer.

Once the oil is hot enough, carefully add the spring rolls in batches and fry for 3–4 minutes, or until golden brown and crispy, turning them occasionally for even cooking. Once cooked, carefully remove the rolls from the oil and transfer to a plate lined with paper towels to drain.

LET'S CHOP!
Serve the suya spring rolls hot, accompanied by sweet chilli sauce or Chilli H'oil.

GUINNESS PORK RIBS

Guinness pork ribs go off!! At all family barbecues this is a real showstopper. We thought a recipe this good should be munched all year round. The richness in flavour, sweet sticky marinade and fall off the bone meat – there is nothing to dislike if you love pork.

2 large racks of pork ribs or 4 smaller ones (weighing around 1.8–2.7 kg/4–6 lb. in total)

juice of 1 large lemon

2 tablespoons Jumbo chicken stock powder (or 2 teaspoons each of salt and dried thyme)

480 ml/2 cups Nigerian Guinness stout

1 tablespoon soft dark brown sugar

120 ml/½ cup soy sauce

1 large garlic clove, crushed/minced

2 tablespoons Dijon mustard

2 tablespoons smoked paprika

2 tablespoons garlic powder

1 tablespoon onion salt

4 tablespoons Worcestershire sauce

6 tablespoons barbecue sauce

salt and freshly ground black pepper

SERVES 4-6 FLY PEOPLE

START WITH THE SEASONING

Preheat the oven to 150°C/300°F/Gas 2.

Wash the pork in a bowl with the fresh lemon juice.

Grab a knife and clean off any excess fat and remove the membrane from the back of the ribs (if present). Rinse under running water, then pat dry. Season the ribs generously with the chicken stock powder.

Mix the Nigerian Guinness, brown sugar, soy sauce, garlic, Dijon mustard, smoked paprika, garlic powder, onion salt, Worcestershire sauce and barbecue sauce together in a bowl.

BAKE IT

Place the seasoned ribs in a large oven tray or baking dish, meaty side up. Pour the Guinness mixture over the ribs, ensuring that they are evenly coated. Leave a cheeky bit of sauce behind so you can baste the ribs as they cook. Cover the oven tray tightly with foil.

Place the ribs in the preheated oven and bake for 3 hours, opening and basting every hour or so, until the meat falls off the bone.

ALMOST TIME TO CHOP

Remove the foil from the oven tray or baking dish, increase the oven temperature to 200°C/400°F/Gas 6, and return the ribs to the oven for 20 minutes to caramelize.

Remove the ribs from the oven and pour the sauce in the tray into a gravy boat to serve with the ribs.

Serve piping hot as there is nothing like making that blowing sound as the ribs melt in your mouth!

ENJOYMENT!

NOTE This is a great side dish that can be enjoyed with the Plantain Fries (see page 103) or Plantain, Halloumi & Walnut Salad (see page 84).

JOLLOF 'ARANCINI'

We created this recipe when trying to use up leftovers at Christmas – there is always that point over the break where you become fed up with eating the same Christmas food. So, we created this recipe to find an inventive way to eat the rest of the seasonal stock.

7 chestnut mushrooms, finely chopped

3 garlic cloves, crushed/minced

1 shallot, finely chopped

4 chives, finely chopped

1 tablespoon dried mixed herbs

500 g/1 lb. 2 oz. leftover Jollof Rice (see page 52)

4 UK medium/US large eggs, beaten

50 g/2 oz. grated Parmesan cheese

a handful of fresh parsley leaves, chopped

125 g/4½ oz. mozzarella cheese, cut into small cubes

500 g/6 cups dried breadcrumbs

1 litre/4 cups vegetable oil, for deep frying, plus extra to sauté the filling

salt

hot sauce of your choice, to serve (optional)

MAKES 10–15 ARANCINI

MAKE THE FILLING

Add a little bit of oil to a frying pan/skillet over a medium heat. Fry the mushrooms, garlic, shallot and chives for 3–4 minutes. Add the mixed herbs, season with salt and stir to combine. Set aside until needed.

MIX IT

In large mixing bowl, mix the leftover jollof rice with 2 of the beaten eggs, the Parmesan and parsley, ensuring the egg has evenly coated the rice and you achieve a sticky texture.

GET SHAPING

Take a small handful of the rice mixture and flatten it in the palm of your hand. Place a cube of mozzarella cheese and a pinch of the mushroom filling in the centre of the flattened patty.

Form a ball with the rice mixture around the stuffing, ensuring that the rice mixture completely seals the filling. Repeat the process with the remaining rice and fillings until it has all been used.

Coat each rice ball thoroughly in the remaining beaten eggs, then evenly cover the coated rice balls with breadcrumbs.

LET'S FRY

Heat the vegetable oil to 180°C/350°F in a deep pan or deep-fat fryer. To test if the oil is ready for frying if you don't have a thermometer, drop a small piece of bread into the pan. If it sizzles and browns straight away, it's ready; if not heat for a little longer.

Fry the coated rice balls in batches for about 3–4 minutes until golden brown and crispy all over. Transfer the fried arancini to a plate lined with paper towels to drain excess oil.

LET'S CHOP!

Serve the arancini hot with hot sauce for dunking, if you like.

ADEGREG STEAK BAKE

This is a fun small chop recipe that we created for our love of Greggs! The steak bake is one of our favourite meals to order at Greggs (the popular British high-street bakery). One of our visions is to make Flygerian food available to everyone as with the popular high-street brand – no matter where you are in the UK, you can always find a cheeky Greggs.

100 ml/scant ½ cup vegetable oil, for frying

200 g/½ cup tomato purée/ paste

2 red Romano peppers, finely diced

1 red Scotch bonnet chilli/chile, diced (or to taste)

1 onion, diced

3 garlic cloves, crushed/minced

500 g/1 lb. 2 oz. beef sirloin steak, finely diced

400-g/14-oz. can chopped tomatoes

320 g/11½ oz. puff pastry sheets

egg wash (beaten egg with a bit of water)

salt and freshly ground black pepper

sweet chilli sauce or Chilli H'oil (see page 19), to serve (optional)

SEASONING

2 tablespoons Jumbo chicken stock

1 tablespoon dried thyme

1 tablespoon curry powder

1 tablespoon smoked paprika

2 tablespoons garlic powder

baking sheet lined with baking parchment

MAKES 5 BAKES

FIRST, MAKE THE FILLING

Preheat the oven to 190°C/375°F/Gas 5.

Place the vegetable oil and tomato purée in a frying pan/skillet over a medium heat. Add the Romano peppers, Scotch bonnet, onion and garlic and sauté until translucent.

Add the steak and all the seasoning to the pan and cook until browned.

Pour in the chopped tomatoes and add salt to taste. Cook for about 10 minutes, allowing the water to evaporate and the sauce to thicken.

MAKE THE BAKES

Cut the pastry into 10 equal-sized rectangles, ensuring you have an even number of sheets.

Spoon the steak mixture onto half the pastry rectangles, leaving some space around the edges.

Top with the remaining pastry rectangles so that the filling is covered and seal the edges by pressing with a fork.

BAKE UNTIL GOLDEN

Place the pastry pockets onto the lined baking sheet and brush the tops with egg wash.

Bake in the preheated oven for 20–25 minutes, or until the pastry is golden brown and flaky. Leave the bakes to cool slightly before serving, accompanied by sweet chilli sauce or Chilli H'oil, if liked.

LET'S CHOP!

2
BIG
CHOPS

FLYGERIAN SMOKY JOLLOF RICE

The staple of every great Nigerian event – if there is no jollof... don't invite us! This traditional party starter is bound to take you on a journey to Nigeria without you ever needing to get on a plane. This smoky flavour will set your jollof apart and comfort you in moments when you never knew you needed it.

400-g/14-oz. can plum tomatoes

1 large red Romano pepper

3 large garlic cloves

2 Scotch bonnet chillies/chiles (or to taste)

2 large onions, 1 for blending and 1 sliced

150 ml/⅔ cup vegetable oil (more can be added if needed to keep it fluffy and light)

100 g/¼ cup tomato purée/ paste

1 kg/2¼ lb. parboiled basmati rice (we always use Tilda Golden Sella basmati rice – see page 16)

salt

SEASONING

1 tablespoon smoked paprika (for extra smokiness)

1 tablespoon garlic powder

2 tablespoons dried thyme

1 tablespoon curry powder (mild, medium or hot)

2 tablespoons Jumbo chicken stock powder or bouillon vegetable powder

2 dried bay leaves

SERVES 4 FLY PEOPLE

FIRST PREPARE THE BASE

Blend the plum tomatoes, Romano pepper, garlic, Scotch bonnets and 1 of the onions in a food processor to a smooth mixture.

Heat the vegetable oil in a large saucepan over a medium heat, add the sliced onion and cook until golden.

Stir in the tomato purée and cook for 10 minutes until it darkens and bubbles. Add the blended mixture, all the seasoning and salt to taste. Cook for about 10 minutes, stirring occasionally, until the oil begins to separate from the tomato mixture.

START WITH THE RICE

Add the rice to the pan and stir until the rice is well-coated with the tomato mixture. Cover with foil and cling film/plastic wrap and cook for 10 minutes.

Remove the foil and cling film and pour in 150 ml/⅔ cup water and mix. Once completely coated with water, cover the pan with foil again and top with the lid. Cook over a low heat for 30 minutes.

TASTE TEST

If the rice is still hard, add a small amount of water and cook for a further 10 minutes. If further seasoning is needed, add more chicken stock or vegetable powder to enhance the flavours.

TURN UP THE HEAT

Once the rice is cooked to your liking, turn up the heat to maximum volume and let the rice burn for 3 minutes to achieve that smoky taste

LET'S CHOP!

Best served hot and scoop from the top to avoid the burned base, unless that's your preference.

TIP The longer the burn, the smokier the taste!

PREMIUM FRIED RICE

'Food should be in abundance' The Flygerians (2020).
We believe that more is more, and that is why our Premium Fried Rice
will make you bring containers to the party.

1 large Spanish onion
3 large garlic cloves
2 sprigs of fresh thyme
a handful of fresh parsley
245 ml/scant 1 cup vegetable oil
1 kg/2¼ lb. parboiled basmati
  rice (see Note below)
2 tablespoons Jumbo chicken
  stock powder or bouillon
  vegetable stock powder

SEASONING
1 tablespoon smoked paprika
1 tablespoon curry powder
  (mild, medium or hot)
1 tablespoon ground turmeric
1 tablespoon dark soy sauce
1 teaspoon ground ginger
1 dried bay leaf

OPTIONAL ADDITIONS
100 g/3½ oz. frozen mixed
  vegetables
100 g/3½ oz. raw king prawns/
  shrimp
50 g/1¾ oz. cold-water prawns/
  shrimp
50 g/1¾ oz. cooked chicken
  breast, diced
20 g/¾ oz. liver
  (cow, beef or chicken)

TO GARNISH (OPTIONAL)
1 spring onion/scallion, chopped
Fried Plantain (see page 33)

SERVES 4-6 FLY PEOPLE

BLEND & PREP TIME

Add the onion, garlic, thyme, parsley and 3 tablespoons of the vegetable oil to a blender and blend to a coarse paste.

Rinse the parboiled rice until the water runs clear.

Heat the remaining vegetable oil in a deep saucepan over a medium heat and add the blended mixture and rice. Mix together well and fry for a few minutes.

STOCK UP

Add the chicken or vegetable stock powder to 150 ml/⅔ cup water, then pour this over the rice.

Add all the seasonings and stir well to ensure even distribution. Cover the rice with foil and steam for 20 minutes over a low heat.

ADD SOME OPTIONAL EXTRAS

Add the frozen mixed vegetables, prawns and diced chicken to the rice, if using, then stir well. If using liver, dice and fry in a separate pan for 5 minutes, then add to the rice mixture and stir well.

IS IT TASTING SWEET?

Taste the fried rice and adjust the seasoning if necessary. You can add more soy sauce or stock powder to your taste. Remove and discard the bay leaf.

LET'S CHOP!

This delicious rice is best eaten hot and can be garnished with spring onions and fried plantain, if liked.

NOTE We like to use parboiled basmati rice as these grains have been parboiled in their husk, which means they retain their texture through the cooking process. We favour Tilda Golden Sella basmati rice (see page 16), but this is usually sold in large bags, so it's good to get stocked up.

SEAFOOD OKRA SOUP

Our seafood okra recipe is a main dish that is normally accompanied by a swallow food of your choosing. It is an immersive experience, best eaten with your hands in the traditional Nigerian way. It can be cooked with assorted meats and fish, but our version here is perfect for pescatarians.

2 white onions, 1 left whole and 1 chopped
4 garlic cloves
1 red Romano pepper
1–2 Scotch bonnet chillies/chiles (or to taste)
650 g/1 lb. 7 oz. fresh okra
550 g/1 lb. 3 oz. assorted seafood (stockfish, king prawns/shrimp, lobster tail and whole crab)
60 g/2 oz. palm oil
100 g/3½ oz. locust beans (iru), rinsed in warm water
100 g/3½ oz. Jumbo prawn/ shrimp stock powder
250 ml/1 cup boiling water
Pounded Yam (see page 88), to serve

SEASONING
1 teaspoon dried thyme
1 teaspoon curry powder (mild, medium or hot)
4 Maggi fish stock cubes
4 teaspoons ground crayfish
salt

SERVES 4-6 FLY PEOPLE

BLEND IT
Add the whole onion, garlic, Romano pepper and Scotch bonnet chillies to a food processor and blend to a coarse texture.

Slice the okra and add to a large bowl. Sprinkle with water and stir until the okra begins to slime.

PREPARE THE ASSORTED SEAFOOD
Deshell (but leave the tails on) and remove the veins from the prawns. The crab can be cooked whole but it is best to partially crack the shell with a mallet. Soak the stockfish in water for 30 minutes.

BRING IT TOGETHER
Heat the palm oil in a large saucepan over a medium heat. Add the chopped onion and locust beans and fry for 2 minutes.

Add the blended mixture to the pan and then all the seasoning. Cook for a further 5 minutes.

Mix the prawn stock powder with the boiling water and stir into the pan. Add the stockfish and cook over a medium heat for 15–20 minutes.

Stir the okra into the pan, then add the lobster tail, crab and prawns and cook for 15 minutes over a low heat.

LET'S CHOP!
Best served hot and with swallow food like pounded yam.

TIPS
» When buying stockfish, ask the fishmonger to cut it into smaller chunks ready for use.

» Palm oil is measured in grams as it is purchased in solid form and will melt as it is heated.

EGUSI SOUP

Egusi soup is one of the most popular Nigerian swallow soups, made from the seeds of a watermelon also known as *Citrullus Lantus*. If the seeds are tasted alone they can be bitter in taste, but with a blend of the finest spices and the blessed wisdom from our ancestors, it creates a cinematic experience in your mouth.

250 g/9 oz. egusi
  (ground melon seeds)
500 g/1 lb 2 oz. assorted meats
  (leg beef, goat, shaki/tripe and
  pomo/cow skin – see page 16),
  cut into bite-sized pieces
5 tablespoons curry powder
  (mild, medium or hot)
5 tablespoons garlic powder
3 tablespoons ground turmeric
3 tablespoons Jumbo beef stock
  powder
2 tablespoons dried thyme
1 red Romano pepper
400-g/14-oz. can plum tomatoes
2–3 Scotch bonnet chillies/chiles
  (or to taste)
2 tablespoons ground crayfish
100 g/3½ oz. palm oil
1 large onion, chopped
200 g/4 cups spinach, chopped
salt

SERVES 4-6 FLY PEOPLE

FIRST, PREPARE THE EGUSI PASTE
Fry the egusi seeds in a dry frying pan/skillet until golden brown, then leave to cool. Once cool, blend to a smooth paste in a food processor or blender.

ADD SOME FLAVOUR
Place the meat in a large saucepan and season with the curry powder, garlic powder, turmeric, beef stock powder, thyme and salt. Add enough boiling water to cover the meat, then cook for about 45 minutes, or until the meat is tender. Keep adding more hot water if needed, as it will go on to be used as stock later.

BRING IT ALL TOGETHER
Place the Romano pepper, plum tomatoes, Scotch bonnets and crayfish powder in a food processor and blend for 30 seconds.

Heat the palm oil in a separate saucepan over a medium heat. Add the onion and sauté until softened, then add the blended pepper mixture. Stir well, then add the egusi paste and cook for 4–5 minutes.

Add 250 ml/1 cup of the meat stock, and the boiled meat to the pan, and add salt to taste.

Lower the heat and cook for 20 minutes, stirring occasionally. Add the chopped spinach and cook for a further 5 minutes.

LET'S CHOP!
Egusi soup is typically served with swallow food like pounded yam, fufu, eba or amala (see pages 88–92).

ONE-POT OGBONO SOUP

Our grandma taught us to cook this dish all in one pot. Why? Because who really enjoys washing up, ha ha. Growing up our grandmother used to serve this dish in a large bowl with a massive side of swallow and we would eat together as a family with our hands. Imagine the challenges of sharing food from the same plate with your family, everyone trying to grab the biggest pieces of meat in the bowl first.

4 kg/8¾ lb. assorted meats (legs of beef, goat meat, shaki/tripe and pomo/cow skin – see page 16)
500 g/1 lb. 2 oz. ground ogbono seeds
2 large white onions, chopped
2 red Romano peppers
2–3 Scotch bonnet chillies/chiles (or to taste)
3 tablespoons ground crayfish (optional)
250 g/9 oz. palm oil
500 g/10 cups spinach
100 g/2 cups fresh bitter leaf (optional)
2 whole fresh mackerel, cleaned and cut into medium-sized chunks.
salt

SEASONING
2 tablespoons paprika
2 tablespoons dried garlic
3 tablespoons Jumbo chicken stock powder
1 tablespoon dried thyme
2 tablespoons curry powder (mild, medium or hot)

SERVES 6-8 FLY PEOPLE

SEASON THE MEAT
Place the assorted meat in a large saucepan and add all the seasoning. Add enough boiling water to submerge the meat and cook for 1 hour, or until tender.

GET BLENDING
Use a spice grinder or mini blender to blend the ogbono seeds to a smooth texture.

Blend the onions, Romano peppers and Scotch bonnets in a blender or food processor to a minced texture.

BRING IT ALL TOGETHER
Add the blended onion mixture, crayfish, if using, and palm oil to the boiling meat and stir well.

Leave to cool for a further 15 minutes, then stir in the blended ogbono. Continue to stir until the ogbono has been thoroughly mixed in, then cook for a further 5 minutes. If the ogbono begins to go lumpy, slowly add boiling water while you are stirring.

FINISHING TOUCHES
Stir in the spinach and bitter leaf, then gently add the raw mackerel to the pan. Place the lid back on the pan and cook over a low heat for 15–20 minutes until the fish is cooked. Once the fish has been placed in the pan don't stir it again as the fish may break apart. Season with salt to taste and enjoy.

BANGA SOUP

Banga is a popular swallow soup from the Igbo tribe, but it's for everyone to chop. Palm oil and palm nut extract (banga) are from different parts of the same fruit. Palm nut extract is the oil derived from the pulp of palm fruit, which gives it an enhanced sweet taste.

1 kg/2¼ lb. assorted dried stockfish

3 kg/6¾ lb. assorted meats (leg beef, goat meat and shaki/tripe – see page 16), chopped into small chunks

2 tablespoons garlic powder

2 tablespoons all-purpose seasoning

1 tablespoon paprika

1 tablespoon turmeric

1 tablespoon mild curry powder

500 ml/2 cups palm nut extract (banga)

1 onion, chopped

4 garlic cloves, crushed/minced

3 Scotch bonnet chillies/chiles (or to taste), chopped

3 tablespoons Jumbo chicken stock powder

200 g/7 oz. fresh bitter leaves

salt

SPICE BLEND

1 onion, chopped

2–3 Scotch bonnet chillies/chiles (or to taste)

1 tablespoon ground crayfish (optional)

1 teaspoon ground uziza seeds (optional)

1 teaspoon ground ogiri or iru (fermented locust beans, optional)

1 tablespoon ground or freshly grated nutmeg

SERVES 4-6
FLY PEOPLE

FIRST, PREPARE THE FISH & MEATS

Soak the stockfish in a bowl of water, ensuring the fish is completely submerged in the water for 30 minutes.

Wash and clean the meat and place it in a large pot. Add the garlic powder, all-purpose seasoning, paprika, turmeric and curry powder and boil for 45–60 minutes, or until the meat is tender.

ADD SOME SPICE

Add all the spice blend ingredients to a blender and blend until smooth.

Place the palm nut extract in a separate large pan over a medium heat. Once the palm extract has melted, add the onion, garlic, Scotch bonnets and chicken stock powder and cook until translucent.

Add the blended spice mixture to the pan and stir well. Cover with the lid and cook for 5 minutes.

Add the cooked meats and soaked stockfish to the soup base, including the stock water.

THICKEN IT UP

Let the banga soup simmer gently for a further 10–15 minutes to allow the flavours to fully develop and the soup to thicken slightly.

Add the bitter leaves and cook for a further 5 minutes. Season to taste with salt – some may think it is salty enough from the chicken stock powder.

LETS CHOP!

Best served hot and with your favourite swallow food (see pages 88–92).

VEGAN EDIKANG IKONG

Edikang Ikong is a traditional leafy Nigerian soup, which we have adapted here to be vegan. We believe food should be for all and there is a growing community of Nigerians who want to eat traditional meals, but without meat. We created this recipe from a love of being inclusive and operating on a 'no one gets left behind policy'.

100 g/3½ oz. locust beans (iru), washed

4 bunches of spinach or Nigerian pumpkin leaves

200 g/7 oz. curly kale

3 tablespoons palm oil or vegetable oil

1 large onion, chopped

4 garlic cloves, crushed/minced

250 g/9 oz. shiitake mushrooms, chopped

1 Scotch bonnet chilli/chile, chopped (optional)

300 g/10½ oz. extra-firm tofu, diced

500 ml/2 cups hot water

2 tablespoons bouillon vegetable stock powder

salt

SEASONING

1 tablespoon dried mixed herbs

1 tablespoon curry powder (mild, medium or hot)

1 tablespoon smoked paprika

1 tablespoon garlic powder

SERVES 4-6 FLY PEOPLE

START SOAKING & WASHING

Soak the locust beans in lukewarm water for 10 minutes, then drain.

Chop the spinach and wash with the kale in a colander. After washing, place in a large mixing bowl lined with paper towels to assist with an extra drain.

GET FRYING

In a large saucepan, heat the palm oil and add the onion, garlic and washed locust beans.

Add the mushrooms, Scotch bonnet, if using, tofu and all the seasoning. Stir well and cook for a few minutes until it starts to brown.

Add the chopped spinach and kale to the pan. Stir well to combine with the other ingredients and add salt to taste.

SIMMER IT DOWN

Pour in the hot water and vegetable stock powder. Turn down the heat and simmer for about 15-20 minutes, or until the vegetables are tender. Taste the soup and adjusting the seasoning, potentially adding more stock powder or salt to taste if needed.

LET'S CHOP!

Best served with swallow food of choice (see pages 88–92), Ofada Rice (see page 88) or plain white rice.

PEPPERED PRAWNS

This prawn/shrimp dish of champions is bursting with vibrant colours and a tantalizing tasty beauty. Our Mum loves this dish and used to make it for us as kids, inspired by her Jamaican best friend, who used to dance round to Beres Hammond with us as she taught us how to make Caribbean-inspired dishes. A sensational blend of spices, and sautéed to perfection, peppered prawns are delicious served as an appetizer or as part of a main course, accompanied by rice, pasta or crusty bread. Enjoy the bold flavours and spicy kick of this tasty dish!

4 tablespoons olive oil or vegetable oil

1 large garlic clove, crushed/minced

1 onion, finely chopped

1 teaspoon grated fresh ginger

1 Scotch bonnet chilli/chile, finely chopped (or to taste)

4 red Romano peppers, chopped

2 tablespoons paprika

1 tablespoon Jumbo prawn/shrimp stock powder

2 sachets of Cock soup (see Note)

2 tablespoons dried thyme

1 tablespoon curry powder (mild, medium or hot)

500 ml/2 cups boiling water

1 kg/2¼ lb. jumbo or large prawns/shrimp, peeled and deveined

2 tablespoons chopped fresh parsley or coriander/cilantro, to garnish

lemon wedges, to garnish

salt

SERVES 2–4 FLY PEOPLE

FRY UP SOME FLAVOUR

Heat the oil in a large pot or deep frying pan/skillet over a medium heat. Add the garlic, onion and ginger and sauté for 2–3 minutes until softened and fragrant.

Add the Scotch bonnet and Romano peppers and sauté for 1 minute. Add the paprika, stock powder, soup sachets, thyme and curry powder and pour in the boiling water.

TASTE TEST

Taste the mixture and add more stock powder and Scotch bonnets for extra flavour if needed.

ADD THE PRAWNS

Stir in the prawns and cook for 3 minutes until the prawns turn pink and opaque. Be careful not to overcook them, they should be juicy and succulent.

LET'S CHOP!

Turn off the heat and transfer the peppered prawns to a serving dish. Garnish with the chopped herbs.

Serve the peppered prawns hot, with lemon wedges on the side for squeezing over, if desired.

NOTE Cock soup sachets, which contain small noodles, can be bought online or from large supermarkets/grocery stores. We use them to add depth to broths.

OXTAIL STEW

This oxtail stew was created out of a love of everything rich in flavour and expensive in price. Oxtail is not meat eaten everyday due to the price point being high as well as the lengthy cooking time needed to tenderize the meat. Therefore, it's usually cooked and served for special occasions. It is best served with plain white rice or Ofada rice (see page 88).

3 kg/6¾ lb. oxtail, trimmed and cut into medium-sized pieces
2 tablespoons white vinegar
2 dashes of lemon juice
2 tablespoons vegetable oil
1 large onion, chopped
5 garlic cloves, crushed/minced
2 teaspoons grated fresh ginger
400-g/14-oz. can chopped tomatoes
200 g/½ cup tomato purée/paste
2 red Romano peppers, chopped
3 Scotch bonnet chillies/chiles, chopped
500 ml/2 cups boiling water
2 tablespoons ground crayfish
1 teaspoon paprika
3 tablespoons Jumbo chicken stock powder
1 tablespoon dried thyme
salt

SERVES 4-6 FLY PEOPLE

PREPARE THE MEAT
Wash the oxtail meat with vinegar and lemon, then sprinkle with salt.

START FRYING
Heat the vegetable oil in a frying pan/skillet, add the onion, garlic, ginger and the oxtail and cook over a medium heat until the meat has browned. Use a slotted spoon to remove the meat and set aside.

Add the chopped tomatoes, tomato purée, Romano peppers and Scotch bonnets to the pan. Cook, stirring occasionally, for 5–7 minutes until the vegetables are softened and the tomatoes break down.

COOK IT LOW & SLOW
Return the browned oxtail to the pan and stir well until the meat and sauce is combined. Add the boiling water to the pan.

Season the stew with the crayfish, paprika, chicken stock powder and thyme and stir well to combine. Bring the stew to a simmer, then slowly stew over a medium heat for 2 hours, or until the meat is tender. Taste and adjust the seasoning.

Best served hot and can be eaten with swallow food (see pages 88–92) or Ofada rice (see page 88).

TIP If the meat is not almost falling off the bone, it needs to be cooked for longer.

AYAMASE STEW

Salute to our Yoruba family. This one is usually made for special occasions, but every day is special right?! Ayamase is a popular Yoruba stew, also known as 'designer stew'. As the traditional recipe requires stamina, we cut out the bleaching of the oil, because we are soft-life babes. This one is for heat lovers, stay clear if you suffer from heartburn or gastric reflux as you might be in for a rough night, ha ha!

3 kg/6¾ lb. assorted meats (cowfoot, shaki/tripe, pomo/cow skin – see page 16)
3 large onions, chopped
4 UK large/US extra-large golden yolk eggs (optional, and any eggs can be used)
15 green (bell) peppers, deseeded and chopped
4 Scotch bonnet chillies/chiles
6 tablespoons Ofada oil (bleached palm oil)
250 g/9 oz. ground crayfish (optional)
1 kg/2¼ lb. dried stockfish
100 g/3½ oz. dried whole prawns/shrimp
salt
Ofada Rice (see page 88), to serve

SEASONING
2 tablespoons Jumbo chicken stock powder
2 tablespoons curry powder (mild, medium or hot)
2 tablespoons garlic powder
2 tablespoons dried thyme
1 tablespoon paprika

SERVES 4-6 FLY PEOPLE

IT'S TIME TO CLEAN
Wash and clean the assorted meats thoroughly and place them in a large saucepan. Add all the seasoning and one of the chopped onions and enough water to submerge the meat. Cook for 1 hour over a medium heat until tender.

Boil the eggs for 10 minutes. Once cooled, peel and set aside.

BLEND IT
In a blender, add the green peppers, Scotch bonnets and one of the chopped onions and blend until smooth.

GET FRYING
Heat the palm oil in a large pan over a medium heat. Add the remaining onion and sauté until translucent. Be careful not to burn it.

Add the blended pepper mixture and stir well. Cook, stirring occasionally, until it reduces and thickens slightly, and the oil begins to separate from the peppers. This usually takes about 10–15 minutes.

LET IT BREW
Add the cooked assorted meats, 250 ml/1 cup of the meat cooking water, the crayfish, stockfish and dried prawns. Stir well to combine with the stew. Cook for a further 10 minutes over a medium heat with the lid off, allowing the water to reduce.

FINISHING TOUCHES
Add salt to taste and extra seasoning if needed – usually the meat stock water will enhance the flavours enough.

If you're adding eggs, place the peeled eggs into the pan and gently stir and cook for a further 10 minutes before serving hot with Ofada Rice, if liked.

VEGAN EFO RIRO SPINACH STEW

Efo Riro is a spinach-based stew that we have adapted for vegans as it is good to give our bodies a break from eating meat sometimes. We serve this recipe in our restaurant because food should be inclusive for everyone. We make it with sustainable palm oil, but it can be adapted with the use of vegetable oil as an alternative.

2 red Romano peppers, chopped
2 red Scotch bonnet chillies/
   chiles
1 large onion, chopped
5 garlic cloves
5 tablespoons palm oil
   (or 100 ml/scant ½ cup
   vegetable oil)
200 g/½ cup tomato purée/
   paste (double concentrated)
400-g/14-oz. can chopped
   tomatoes
2.5 kg/5½ lb. frozen spinach

SEASONING
2 tablespoons mild curry powder
2 tablespoons paprika
1 tablespoon dried thyme
3 tablespoons bouillon
   vegetable stock powder
2 Maggi vegetable stock cubes
salt

SERVES 4-6 FLY PEOPLE

START WITH BLENDING
Using a food processor, blend the Romano peppers, Scotch bonnets, onion and garlic cloves to a coarse paste.

FRY THE BASE
Heat the palm oil or vegetable oil in a large saucepan over a medium heat. Add the blended mixture and tomato purée to the pan and fry for 2–3 minutes, stirring well to ensure the oil is distributed evenly.

Stir in the chopped tomatoes, add all the seasoning and stir well until combined. Cook for 15 minutes.

ADD SOME GREENS
Slowly stir the spinach into the pan until combined. Partially cover and let the spinach cook for about 5–7 minutes, or until wilted and tender, over a low heat.

Taste and adjust the seasoning if needed, adding more salt or spices according to your preference.

LET'S CHOP!
Best served with swallow food but can be eaten with white rice and Agege Bread (see page 23).

TIP Using frozen spinach gives a better finish to this recipe.

ONE-POT PEPPERED GOAT MEAT

This dish should be served piping hot and is delicious with our Ofada rice (see page 88), plain white rice, boiled yam or boiled plantain.

2 kg/4½ lb. goat meat, excess fat removed and cut into small chunks

3 tablespoons Jumbo chicken stock powder

1 tablespoon dried thyme

1 tablespoon curry powder (mild, medium or hot)

2 tablespoons garlic powder

1 tablespoon paprika

4 tablespoons vegetable oil

1 large onion, chopped

1 small garlic clove, crushed/minced

2 tablespoons grated fresh ginger

6 tablespoons tomato purée/paste

4–6 Scotch bonnet chillies/chiles, finely chopped

4 large (bell) peppers (2 red, 1 green, 1 yellow)

salt and freshly ground black pepper

fresh parsley, to garnish (optional)

SERVES 3-6 FLY PEOPLE

FIRST, PREPARE THE MEAT

Wash the pieces of goat meat in a bowl of cold water. Repeat this 3 times, then pat dry.

Place the meat in a large bowl and season with the chicken stock powder, thyme, curry powder, garlic powder and paprika. Combine until all the meat is covered evenly. Leave it to marinate overnight to give the goat meat maximum flavour. If you're in a hurry, 1 hour will do.

START FRYING

Heat the oil in a large frying pan/skillet over a medium-high heat. Add the marinated goat meat chunks in batches and brown them on all sides, adding more oil if needed. Set aside the browned meat.

Add the onion, garlic and ginger to the same pan over a low heat and sauté until the onions are soft.

Stir in the tomato purée and the Scotch bonnets and cook for a few minutes to develop the flavours, then cook over a low heat for about 15–20 minutes. The paste should turn darker in colour.

COOK IT SLOW

Return the browned meat to the pan and mix into the onion mixture. Pour in enough water to just cover the meat. Keep over a low heat and cover the pan with foil and then a lid. The meat should cook and soften for about 1–2 hours until tender. Check occasionally and add more water and chicken stock powder if needed. Don't let the meat dry out, so top up with more water as needed.

FINAL TOUCHES

Once cooked, add the peppers and cook for a further 15 minutes.

Once the meat is tender and the sauce has thickened, taste and adjust the seasoning with salt and pepper if needed. Garnish with parsley, if using.

CHOP IT!

JOLLOF SPAGHETTI

Growing up we used to ask our Mum for 'spag bol' and this is what she produced. Rather than an Italian blend of flavours, the spaghetti we used to eat tasted like jollof. With the surge of the internet mixing with first generation Nigerians born in the UK we began to realize that most of our parents' spaghetti tasted just like jollof. Once a funny joke we used to laugh about, has now become a staple dish cooked in our home. This recipe brings us back to our childhood and all the shared meals we had with our siblings.

1 tablespoon olive oil

250 g/9 oz. dried spaghetti

1 tablespoon Jumbo chicken stock powder or bouillon vegetable stock

3 tomatoes

3 red (bell) peppers

2 onions, 1 chopped and 1 blended

1 small Scotch bonnet chilli/chile (or to taste)

3 tablespoons vegetable oil

1 garlic bulb, crushed/minced

1 teaspoon grated fresh ginger

1 teaspoon paprika

1 teaspoon curry powder (mild, medium or hot)

½ teaspoon dried thyme

½ teaspoon dried basil (optional)

3 tablespoons tomato purée/ paste

salt and freshly ground black pepper

chopped fresh parsley, to garnish (optional)

SERVES 2-3 FLY PEOPLE

START WITH THE SPAGHETTI

Bring a large pot of salted water to the boil and add the olive oil. Add the spaghetti and cook according to the package instructions until al dente. Drain, reserving 250 ml/1 cup of pasta cooking water. Put the cooked spaghetti in a large bowl and set aside until needed.

Mix the chicken or vegetable stock powder with 150 ml/⅔ cup of the reserved pasta water.

MAKE SOME FLAVOUR

Put the tomatoes, red pepper, 1 of the onions and the Scotch bonnet in a food processor or blender and blend to a smooth texture.

CREATE THE BASE

Heat the vegetable oil in a deep saucepan, and sauté the chopped onion, garlic and ginger for 2–3 minutes.

Pour in the blended mixture and season with the paprika, chicken or vegetable stock, curry powder, thyme, basil and salt. Let it cook for a further 3 minutes over a low heat.

Add the drained spaghetti to the pan. Gently turn and massage the spaghetti through the sauce, making sure the pasta is fully covered in your delicious jollof sauce.

LOOSEN IT UP

Use the remaining pasta water to loosen the sauce should it need it and season to taste with salt and pepper. Garnish with parsley, if using, and enjoy.

NAIJA FISH 'N' CHIPS

Fish Friday is a tradition in our household; we love fish and chips. However, growing up, cod was not a familiar fish cooked in our kitchen. Combining our two beautiful cultures, we created this lightly battered recipe to complement our Naija (the abbreviation for Nigeria) take on this popular British takeaway. Garnished with sautéed peppers with a kick of heat and best served hot, enjoy with a side of chips/fries.

2 red bream fish, heads removed

freshly squeezed juice of 1 lemon

2 tablespoons paprika

2 tablespoons garlic powder

2 tablespoons Jumbo fish stock powder

3 tablespoons dried mixed herbs

1 tablespoon curry powder (mild, medium or hot)

2 eggs, any size

250 g/2½ cups cornflour/cornstarch

vegetable oil, for deep frying

SAUTÉED PEPPERS

100 ml/scant ½ cup vegetable oil

3 mixed (bell) peppers, finely sliced (1 red, 1 yellow, 1 green)

1 large onion, finely sliced

1 Scotch bonnet chilli/chile, chopped

2 garlic cloves, finely chopped

1 tablespoon Jumbo fish stock powder

1 tablespoon garlic powder

1 tablespoon paprika

1 tablespoon dried mixed herbs

salt

SERVES 4 FLY PEOPLE

SALT BAE

Sprinkle the fish with a little of the lemon juice and use a knife to scrape against the skin, removing excess scales and guts. Cut each fish into 3 chunks and place in a large mixing bowl.

Season the fish with the paprika, garlic powder, fish stock powder, mixed herbs, curry powder and 2 tablespoons of the lemon juice. Ensure the fish is evenly covered, then leave the fish to marinate for about 30 minutes.

LET'S MAKE THE BATTER

In a large bowl, whisk the eggs. In a separate bowl, sift the cornflour.

Firstly, dip the fish chunks in the egg, then evenly coat with cornflour and set aside to fry. Repeat this method until all the fish is battered.

FRY IT UP!

Fill a deep saucepan halfway with vegetable oil and heat to 180°C/350°F. Once the oil is hot, place the fish chunks in the pan and fry for 4 minutes on each side. Transfer to paper towels to drain any excess oil.

In a separate pan, heat the vegetable oil, and add the sliced peppers, onion, Scotch bonnet and garlic. Stir well and season with the fish stock powder, garlic powder, paprika and mixed herbs. Stir for about 5 minutes and add salt to taste.

Serve the crispy fried fish with the sautéed peppers.

TIP when purchasing the fish, ask the fish monger to descale and removed the guts, or you can do this yourself.

ROAST LAMB FLYGERIAN STYLE

This is the perfect dish for a Sunday roast or a special occasion. Cooked to perfection, this dish will always be a favourite and will fill your soul with joy.

1 large lamb shank (weighing about 340–450 g/12–16 oz.)

juice of 1 lemon

100 ml/scant ½ cup olive oil

6 tablespoons paprika

4 tablespoons curry powder (mild, medium or hot)

2 tablespoons ground cumin

2 tablespoons ground cinnamon

4 tablespoons Jumbo chicken stock powder (or to taste)

4 tablespoons garlic powder

1 tablespoon ground turmeric

1 large Spanish onion, finely chopped (or 3 medium onions)

400-g/14-oz can plum tomatoes

1–2 Scotch bonnet chillies/chiles (or other chillies), finely chopped (or to taste)

2 large garlic cloves, crushed/ minced

4 large red Romano peppers, chopped

2 tablespoons vegetable oil

2.5-cm/1-inch piece of fresh ginger, grated

2 tablespoons tomato purée/ paste

2 tablespoons honey

salt

fresh parsley, to garnish (optional)

SERVES 2–4 FLY PEOPLE

START THE LONG MARINADE

Wash the lamb with lemon juice and remove any excess fat. Once washed, pat dry with paper towels and place on a clean baking sheet. Poke holes in the lamb leg with a skewer or sharp knife.

Mix half the olive oil with 4 tablespoons of the paprika, half the curry powder, the cumin and cinnamon, half the chicken stock powder, the garlic powder, turmeric and salt to taste in a bowl. Massage the mixture into the lamb and leave it to marinade for 24 hours or at least 4 hours – the longer it's left to marinade the deeper the flavour.

COOK IT SLOW

Preheat the oven to 180–190°C/350–375°F/Gas 4–5. Cover the tray with foil and cook slowly for 2–3 hours until the lamb is tender.

Add half the onion, the plum tomatoes, Scotch bonnet, half the garlic and the Romano peppers to a processor or blender and blend until almost smooth – we like to keep a bit of texture.

FRY IT UP

Heat the vegetable oil in a large pot or Dutch oven over a medium heat. Add the remaining onion and garlic and sauté for about 2–3 minutes until softened and translucent.

Stir in the ginger and sauté for a further 1–2 minutes until fragrant. Add the tomato purée and cook for 3–4 minutes.

Pour the blended mixture into the pot and season with the remaining paprika, curry powder and chicken stock powder, adding more to your taste if wanted.

Add the honey and salt to taste and cook for 30 minutes until the sauce has thickened slightly. Turn off and check on the lamb. We love it pink but you can cook it until well done if you like and cook for another hour.

LET'S CHOP!

Get a clean serving plate, grab a sharp knife and slice the lamb. Top with the sweet pepper stew. You can also debone the lamb and mix it into the stew and serve while hot for maximum enjoyment. Garnish with fresh parsley, if using.

WARM PLANTAIN, HALLOUMI & WALNUT SALAD

When we say this simple recipe will have you wanting to praise the most high... we mean it! It's refreshing, moreish and a beautiful accompaniment to our Guinness Pork Ribs (see page 44), Supermalt Wings (see page 37) and Plantain Fries (see page 103), or on its own as a light snack.

2 ripe plantains, peeled
200 ml/scant 1 cup olive oil
200 ml/¾ cup honey
140 g/½ cup chopped walnuts
150 g/4 cups mixed salad greens, washed
30 g/¼ cup crumbled halloumi
35 g/¼ cup dried raisins or cranberries (optional)
30 g/¼ cup finely sliced red onion (optional)

DRESSING
2 tablespoons olive oil
juice of 1 small lemon
1 tablespoon honey
1 teaspoon salt
1 teaspoon cayenne pepper (or more to taste)
2 tablespoons balsamic vinegar

baking sheet lined with baking parchment or foil

SERVES 2-4 FLY PEOPLE

START WITH THE PLANTAINS
Preheat the oven to 200°C/400°F/Gas 6.

Slice the plantains, then cut each slice in half or into four chunks, depending on your preference.

ROAST IT
Place the plantain chunks on the lined baking sheet, making sure they are evenly spaced and not overlapping. Drizzle all over with the olive oil. Bake for 5 minutes, then flip the chunks. Add the honey and walnuts and cook for a further 10 minutes. Remove from the heat and leave to cool.

Place the greens in a large bowl, add the halloumi, roasted plantain and walnuts, and toss in the raisins or cranberries and red onion, if using.

MAKE A DRESSING
Once all combined, grab a small bowl to make a dressing. Mix all the dressing ingredients together well, then pour onto the salad and toss to mix.

LET'S CHOP!
Once the salad has been tossed, it's time to chop.

TIP If you want to spice this dish up and distribute the sweetness, roast a raw aubergine/eggplant, cut into chunks, to the baking sheet with the plantain.

3
SWALLOW & SIDES

OFADA RICE

Ofada rice is a type of locally grown rice in Nigeria with a distinct aroma, flavour and slightly sticky texture. It's often characterized by its brownish-red or unpolished appearance, with some grains having dark spots. Ofada rice is typically cultivated in the Ogun State of Nigeria and derives its name from the town of the same name. It is traditionally served alongside a spicy stew known as Ayamase (see page 70). This is our Dad's favourite rice.

500 g/2½ cups ofada rice
  (Nigerian brown rice)
2 tablespoons salted butter
  (optional, vegan alternatives
  can be used)
250 ml/1 cup boiling water
salt (optional)

SERVES 2-4 FLY PEOPLE

RINSE & RINSE AGAIN
Place the ofada rice in a large bowl and cover with lukewarm water. Using your hands, swirl the rice and drain off the cloudy water. Repeat this process 3–4 times, until the water runs clear. This helps to remove excess starch and impurities from the rice.

Boil the washed rice in a saucepan of water for 10 minutes, then drain.

LET'S SERVE UP
Melt the butter in a separate pan over a medium heat. Once the butter has melted, add the rice, boiling water and salt to taste, if liked. Cover the pot and allow to cook for a further 15 minutes. Ensuring the rice is cooked to your desired texture, adding water if it still has a bite.

Best served with Ayamase (see page 70).

POUNDED YAM

Pounded yam is a staple Nigerian dish that we like to refer to as 'Nigerian mashed potato', but better. There is no pounding in our recipe though; we are boujie. It has a smooth taste when blended well and goes beautifully with Efo Riro Stew (see page 71), Ogbono Soup (see page 60) and Seafood Okra Soup (see page 56). We remember wholesome moments spent using elbow grease and all our might, standing on our little stool, and taking it in turns to stir when our mama (Grandma) would let us, and then helping her dish up to serve our cousins. Just before she'd let us pick a movie and we would snuggle up into the sofa or in any space left on the carpet and reach for the food. We always ate together and it is these memories we'll never forget.

2 large yams
salt

SERVES 3-6 FLY PEOPLE

PREPARE THE YAMS
Using a sharp knife, peel the skin off the yam, then cut into medium-sized chunks.

Add the chunks of yam to a large saucepan of boiling water, add a pinch of salt and cook for 20 minutes or until soft.

Drain the yam in a colander and leave to stand for 5 minutes.

LET'S BUNDLE & SERVE IT UP
Add the cooked yam to a food processor and blend until smooth.

Mould into a rounded shape and serve with your favourite soup or stew.

EBA

Eba is a traditional swallow dish made from garri, which is a granulated flour made from cassava. Eba was our grandmother's favourite swallow dish because she loved Gary from *Eastenders* (a British TV programme). She found it humorous that a person could be named 'Gary' as she associated this name with food. It is traditionally eaten with most popular Nigerian soups – Seafood Okra (see page 56), Ogbono (see page 60) and Egusi (see page 59). If you want your presentation to look on-point or Instagram-able, place cooked eba in clingfilm/plastic wrap, mould into shape, then unwrap before serving.

2 tablespoons palm oil (optional)
500 g/1 lb. 2 oz. garri
   (granulated cassava)
salt

SERVES 2 FLY PEOPLE

SOFTEN THE PALM OIL
Add 750 ml/3 cups cold water to a medium-size saucepan or pot with a lid and bring to the boil.

Turn the heat down to a low simmer, then add the palm oil to the boiling water, if using, and add some salt. Stir well.

THICKEN IT UP
Add the garri and stir until the mixture thickens (preferably using a wooden spoon).

Cover the pot with the lid and turn off the heat. Allow the garri to sit for 5 minutes then continue to stir until it begins to form a stiff dough.

Allow to sit for a further 5 minutes then prepare to serve with your favourite soup.

AMALA

Amala is a traditional Nigerian swallow food made from yam flour. Dark in appearance you'd presume it would be bitter but in fact we find it sweet in taste. To prepare amala from scratch takes time and we prefer the soft life. You can purchase the amala yam flour from many African food wholesalers and this recipe is our family secret to achieving a smooth texture. This method can be physically demanding, so get ready to work that upper body. Amala is best served hot and with traditional soups like Egusi (see page 59) or Seafood Okra (see page 56). Traditionally, amala is eaten with your hands but a spoon can be used.

500 g/3½ cups amala yam flour
250 ml/1 cup boiling water
salt

SERVES 1-2 FLY PEOPLE

START THE DOUGH
Using a large mixing bowl, add 500 ml/2 cups cold water to the amala and whisk in the water until you have a smooth consistency.

Add the boiling water to a large saucepan, then slowly stir in the amala and water mixture.

FORMATION
Cook the mixture over a low heat and continue to stir for about 5 minutes until the amala has thickened. If the mixture appears to be lumpy add a few drops of boiling water and continue to stir to smooth it out.

TIP use a wooden spoon when mixing to achieve the best consistency.

PLANTAIN FUFU

Plantain fufu is a recipe we created when looking for healthier and less starchy swallow food. This can be eaten with Nigerian soups like Ogbono (see page 60), Seafood Okra (see page 56) and Egusi (see page 59).

3 ripe green plantains
salt

SERVES 2–3 FLY PEOPLE

PREPARE THE PLANTAIN
Peel and rinse the plantains, then cut into small chunks. .

Place the plantain chunks into a blender and add 250 ml/1 cup cold water, then blend until smooth.

LET'S GET COOKING
Pour the blended mixture into a saucepan and begin to cook over a medium heat.

Stir continuously until the plantain mixture has thickened and add salt to taste. This process usually takes 5–10 minutes.

TIME TO CHOP
Plantain fufu is best served hot and with your desired soup.

BUTTERY CASSAVA MASH

This recipe is the West African answer to mashed potatoes. It's perfect eaten as a side dish with sausages, a stew or a roast dinner. It is best served hot and garnished with chives.

5 large cassava
   (about 5 kg/11 lb.)
2 teaspoons butter
   or vegan spread
salt and freshly ground
   black pepper
a few snipped chives,
   to garnish (optional)

SERVES 2–4 FLY PEOPLE

PREPARE THE CASSAVA
Peel the cassava and cut them into small chunks, then rinse thoroughly.

Add the cassava chunks to a large saucepan of boiling salted water, then cook until tender (test by piercing with a fork). It's always best to overcook rather than undercook cassava.

LET'S MASH
Drain the cooked cassava in a colander, ensure all the excess water has drained off. Tip the cassava back into the pan, then use a potato masher to break down the flesh.

Add the butter or spread and season to taste with salt and pepper. Beat the ingredients with the cassava until it is well mashed and lump free.

LETS CHOP!
Best served hot and garnished with fresh chives, if liked.

NOTE Cassava should never be eaten raw.

4
STREET
FOOD

DON'T BE BASIC
INDOMIE NOODLES

This recipe was created while we were at university and were looking to upgrade basics to recipes to suit our boujie personalities. Indomie instant noodles are produced in Indonesia but Nigeria has become one of the biggest consumers of these fabulous noodles. They are loved on the street food scene in Nigeria and known as the 'designer noodles' as each person can customize their noodles with whatever it is they like. This a beautiful party in your mouth from a cheap eat that feels like it should cost more. They were our go-to food when our parents were too tired from work to cook as children, and also a uni favourite when we only had £5 in our pockets until the student loan dropped. This snack/meal reminds us of humble beginnings and our childhood running to our fridge to grab all the best toppings to create a meal better than our siblings.

2 x 80-g/3-oz. packs of Indomie Mi Goreng stir-fry noodles
2 teaspoons vegetable oil
1 small white onion, diced
1 teaspoon Shito (Ghanaian hot pepper sauce, see page 20) or chilli/chili oil
2 garlic cloves, thinly sliced
3 chestnut mushrooms, thinly sliced
1 red (bell) pepper, deseeded and finely chopped
1 red Scotch bonnet chilli/chile, finely chopped
50 g/1¾ oz. mange tout/snow peas

6 baby corn
1 tablespoon soy sauce
1 teaspoon ground ginger
a handful of baby leaf spinach
salt

OPTIONAL EXTRAS
1 cooked sausage (chicken, beef or vegan frankfurter), diced
150 g/5½ oz. cold water prawns/shrimp

TO GARNISH
2 spring onions/ scallions, diced
a handful of fresh coriander/cilantro leaves, chopped

SERVES 2 FLY PEOPLE

NOODLE TIME
Cook the noodles as per the instructions on the pack, then set aside until needed.

WOK IT
Using a wok or deep frying pan/skillet, heat the vegetable oil, then add the onion, shito and garlic and fry until softened and translucent.

Add the mushrooms, red pepper, Scotch bonnet, mange tout, baby corn, soy sauce and ginger and stir-fry for 2 minutes.

BRING IT ALL TOGETHER
Combine the cooked noodles in the pan with the vegetable mix, ensuring the vegetables and noodles are mixed evenly.

Add the spinach and cooked sausage or prawns, if using. Stir to wilt the spinach and warm the sausage or prawns through.

LET'S CHOP!
This dish is best served hot and can be garnished with chopped spring onions and fresh coriander.

LEKKI EXPRESS NIGERIAN SHAWARMA

This recipe is our adaptation of the traditional shawarma that was constructed while staying in Lekki, Lagos. This recipe has been inspired by our love for Middle Eastern food and culture. While adhering to the basic recipe, we have added our Flygerian twist to it. If you have ever tried a Nigerian-style shawarma you would have observed this bizarre need to have frankfurters in a lot of our meals. So, sticking to our traditions here's our shawarma recipe with optional frankfurter. Lekki Express Shawarma is best served hot but can be eaten cold. It can be served as a small chop or main, accompanied by Twice-cooked Cassava Chips (see page 100) or French fries.

500 g/1 lb. 2 oz. boneless chicken thighs, cut into strips (or lamb leg or shoulder)

SHAWARMA MARINADE
4 tablespoons mayonnaise
2 tablespoons plain/natural yogurt
2 garlic cloves
1 tablespoon cayenne pepper
2 tablespoons lemon juice
1 tablespoon smoked paprika
1 teaspoon ground cumin
1 tablespoon onion powder
2 tablespoons Jumbo chicken stock powder
salt and freshly ground black pepper

TO SERVE
chilli/chili oil, to drizzle
garlic mayonnaise
your favourite burger sauce
4–6 large flour tortilla wraps, warmed
1 large red onion, thinly sliced
1 large tomato, thinly sliced
1 large cucumber, thinly sliced
shredded crunchy lettuce
shredded red cabbage
gherkins, thinly sliced (optional)
1 frankfurter per wrap (optional)

SERVES 4-6 FLY PEOPLE

START WITH THE MARINADE
In a large mixing bowl, combine the shawarma marinade ingredients.

Add the chicken thighs or lamb, cover and place in the fridge to marinate for 1 hour.

ROAST IT UP
Preheat the oven to 200°C/400°F/Gas 6.

Place the marinated meat in a roasting pan and cook in the preheated oven for 15–20 minutes until thoroughly cooked. (Alternatively you can use an air fryer if you have one – set it to 'grill mode' at 200°C/400°F.)

Cook the frankfurters as per the package instructions, if using.

LET'S WRAP
Spread the chilli oil, garlic mayo and burger sauce on the warmed tortilla wraps. Add a layer of meat, followed by the sliced onions, tomatoes, cucumber, shredded lettuce and red cabbage, plus gherkins or frankfurters, if using.

Wrap the filled tortilla using foil to help keep everything intact and slice in half.

TWICE-COOKED CASSAVA CHIPS

Our Grandma used to host annual barbecues also known as 'Mamas cookouts' that would bring together neighbours, family, friends and any stranger who just happened to be strolling past and wanted in on the action! Everyone knew who she was because you could smell her food from miles away. A recipe that is perfect for any get-together is our signature, simple-yet-tasty 'naughty pot' of twice-cooked cassava chips/fries.

6 large cassava
vegetable oil, for deep frying
sea salt and cracked black
    pepper
sliced spring onions/scallions,
    to garnish
Chilli H'oil (see page 19),
    to serve

a deep-fat fryer (optional)

SERVES 3-4 FLY PEOPLE

FIRST, PREP THE CASSAVA

Rinse the cassava skin, as it is usually waxed. Peel off the skin with a sharp knife or potato peeler and cut into chunky chip-sized batons.

Bring a large saucepan of water to the boil and drop in the cassava batons. Boil for 20 minutes or until soft. You can test the cassava's softness by using a fork – the fork should easily pierce through when pressed into a chunk.

Using a colander drain the cassava and shake to create a rustic, uneven texture on the surface. Leave it to sit in the colander for 10 minutes to ensure the excess water has fully drained off.

GET READY TO FRY

Set up and heat your deep-fat fryer, if using, to 180°C/350°F or add sufficient vegetable oil to a large deep-sided saucepan. If using a pan, fill with oil no higher than mid-way to avoid any hot oil splashing back at you.

Place a batch of prepared cassava in the hot oil and fry for 5–6 minutes or until a light golden colour. When cooked, tip onto a plate lined with paper towels to drain the excess oil.

ADD SOME FLAVOUR

Season with salt and a few grinds of cracked black pepper and garnish with the sliced spring onions. Serve hot with the Chilli H'oil on the side.

PLANTAIN FRIES
DODO CHIPS

Plantain fries are a delicious alternative to everyday fries, acting as a sweet, delicious side dish to be chopped with any of our stews – meat or vegan – or they can be chopped on their own. So simple, yet delicious.

4 medium ripe plantains
200 g/2 cups cornflour/
   cornstarch
500 ml/2 cups vegetable oil,
   for deep frying
salt and freshly ground black
   pepper

SWEET BELL PEPPER
DIPPING SAUCE
1 garlic clove, peeled and
   chopped
½ Scotch bonnet chilli/chile
   (use a whole one or even two
   for a slightly spicier hit)
2 white onions, diced
400-g/14-oz. can chopped
   tomatoes
3 red Romano peppers, chopped
150 ml/⅔ cup vegetable oil,
   for frying
2 tablespoons tomato purée/
   paste
1 vegetable stock cube,
   crumbled
1 tablespoon paprika
1 tablespoon curry powder
   (mild, medium or hot)
1 tablespoon dried thyme
salt

SERVES 2-4 FLY PEOPLE

LET'S GET PEELING!
Peel the plantains and cut them into thin slices, about 5 mm–1 cm/ ¼–½ inch thick. You can slice them diagonally or straight, as you prefer. Put them in a bowl once cut into chip-shape fingers.

Grab a bowl and pour in the cornflour, grab a clean plate.

Dip the plantain fries into the cornflour and stack up on your plate.

START THE FRYING
Heat the vegetable oil in a deep frying pan/skillet or a pot on medium-high heat until it reaches about 180–190°C/350–375°F and feels hot to be near... do not touch!

Gently add the plantain slices to the hot oil in batches for no more than 4 minutes until golden and crispy. Scoop them out using a slotted spoon and place them on paper towels to get rid of excess oil.

Let's get some basic seasoning on those beauties, add some salt and pepper to taste.

LET'S MAKE THE DIPPING SAUCE
Grab a blender and add the garlic, Scotch bonnet, half the diced onion, chopped tomatoes and Romano peppers and pulse. You want the sauce to have texture so even slight lumps are great.

Add the oil to a saucepan. Add the remaining diced onion, tomato purée, stock cube, paprika, curry powder, thyme and a pinch of salt. Cook over a medium heat until the purée darkens, then add the blended Romano pepper and tomato mixture. Cook over a low heat for 30 minutes, stirring after 15 minutes.

Serve the hot fries with the dipping sauce on the side.

THE MOMENT YOU'VE BEEN WAITING FOR – ENJOYMENT!

OKRA FRIES

Okra fries is a dish we created when trying to be kind to our waistline and reduce our carb intake. They are a good substitute to chips/fries when looking at healthier options for a side dish. Here we opted to fry the okra pods in oil but you can be kind to your body by using an air fryer. Okra fries can be eaten with any condiment you like, but we prefer ketchup and mayo.

vegetable oil, for deep frying
1 kg/2¼ lb. fresh okra
1 tablespoon salt
2 tablespoons smoked paprika
2 tablespoons garlic powder
2 tablespoons dried mixed herbs
1 tablespoon freshly ground
  black pepper
2 teaspoons olive oil
250 g/2½ cups cornflour/
  cornstarch

SERVES 2-4 FLY PEOPLE

TURN UP THE HEAT
Heat the oil in a large, deep frying pan/skillet while you prepare the okra. Wash the okra in cold water, then cut the top and bottom off each pod.

Place the washed okra in a large bowl add the salt, smoked paprika, garlic powder, mixed herbs, black pepper and olive oil. Use your hands or a wooden spoon to mix in the seasonings.

FRY AWAY
Place the cornflour in a separate bowl and dip the seasoned okra into the flour mixture one at a time. Ensure the okra pods are evenly covered with the cornflour mixture and continue this method until all okra pods are battered.

Gently place the battered okra in the hot oil and fry for 5 minutes, until they appear golden brown.

LETS CHOP!
Drain the excess of oil with sheets of paper towel and serve hot.

TIP If the okra are particularly slippy, you can dip them in beaten egg or vegetable oil to help the cornflour stick and coat them thoroughly.

NIGERIAN BEEF 'MEAT' PIES

If there is no meat pie, don't invite us ooooooh! This street food staple is one of our family favourites. There is nothing more mouthwatering than the buttery pastry that falls apart with every bite. Walking through the streets of Lagos you are never far away from a bringer of joy – a meat pie seller.

2 tablespoons vegetable oil
1 white onion, finely chopped
2 garlic cloves, crushed/minced
300 g/10½ oz. minced/ground beef
1 teaspoon garlic powder
1 tablespoon smoked paprika
2 tablespoons Jumbo chicken stock powder
1 tablespoon dried thyme
1 teaspoon mild curry powder
2 dried bay leaves
1 large potato, diced into small cubes and boiled
1 carrot, diced
1 egg, beaten (for egg wash)

PASTRY
500 g/3¾ cups plain/all-purpose flour, plus extra for dusting
1 teaspoon baking powder
½ teaspoon salt
250 g/2¼ sticks cold butter (or margarine), cubed
500 ml/2 cups cold water (you might not need all of it)

10–12.5-cm/4–5-inch round cookie cutter
baking sheet lined with baking parchment

MAKES 6-8 PIES

FIRST, MAKE THE PASTRY
Preheat the oven to 180°C/350°F/Gas 4.

Mix the flour, baking powder and salt in a large mixing bowl. Add the cold cubed butter and, using your hands, gently rub it into the flour mixture until it resembles large breadcrumbs. Rub your hands together to remove the clumped mixture stuck to your fingers.

A little at a time, slowly add cold water with one hand, and mix with the other until the dough comes together. Be careful not to over knead the dough and don't add too much water. Once it forms a ball, cover the bowl with cling film/plastic wrap and pop it in the fridge for at least 30 minutes while you prepare the filling.

SORT THAT FILLING OUT
Set a frying pan/skillet over a medium heat and once hot, add the vegetable oil, then the onion and garlic. Sauté until soft. Add the beef, garlic powder, paprika, chicken stock powder, thyme, curry powder and bay leaves. Cook for 15–20 minutes until the meat browns, breaking it up with a spoon as it cooks. Slowly stir in the potato and carrot. Cover the pan and cook for 10 minutes. Remove the pan from the heat, remove and discard the bay leaves and leave the filling to cool.

FORM THE PIES
Dust a clean surface with flour and roll out the chilled pastry to 5 mm/¼ inch thick. Use the cookie cutter to cut out 6–8 circles of dough.

Place 1½ tablespoons of the meat filling onto one half of each dough circle, leaving a gap around the edges. Add a drop of water to your finger and rub it round the sides of the unfilled pastry. Fold the dough over the filling to create a half-moon shape and use a fork to crimp the edges to seal tightly.

Place the assembled meat pies on the lined baking sheet. Brush the tops with beaten egg for a golden finish. Bake in the preheated oven for 25–30 minutes, or until the meat pies are golden brown and cooked through. Leave to cool slightly before serving.

NAIJA PLANTAIN & SLOW-COOKED TACOS

A standing ovation for this beauty. If you love tacos and plantain as much as we do, you're about to cry tears of joy after making this one. Our love for plantain is unmatched and this was a dish we created out of our love for tacos and a need to give them a Flygerian twist! We're talking Mexico meeting Nigeria in sweet harmony and pure bliss. If you love it spicy, add an extra Scotch bonnet, or if you like make it three, but warning, it's not for the faint hearted! We personally recommend one so that the heat isn't overpowering. You can cook this in an electric slow cooker if you have one, or in the oven in a lidded casserole/Dutch oven if preferred.

1 kg/ 2¼ lb. beef boneless leg chunks or braising beef
2 tablespoons Jumbo chicken stock powder or 2 beef stock cubes (we have found chicken stock makes it sweeter)
3 tablespoons olive oil
2 white onions, chopped
1 large garlic clove, crushed/minced
400-g/14-oz. can chopped tomatoes
1 small Scotch bonnet chilli/chile, finely chopped
3 red Romano peppers
2 tablespoons smoked paprika
2 tablespoons garlic powder
1 tablespoon curry powder (mild, medium or hot) (or more to taste)
1 tablespoon dried thyme
salt and freshly ground black pepper

PLANTAIN TACO SHELLS
4 large plantains, peeled and each cut into 3 chunks of equal size
1 tablespoon salt (or more to taste)
3 tablespoons plain/all-purpose flour, plus extra for dusting
about 250 ml/1 cup vegetable oil, for shallow frying

TO SERVE
shredded crunchy lettuce
sour cream or crème fraiche
finely diced red onion
finely chopped coriander/cilantro
250 g/2½ cups grated Cheddar cheese
lime wedges, for squeezing

slow cooker (optional)
taco press (optional)

SERVES 2-4 FLY PEOPLE

START WITH SOME SEASONING

Season the beef chunks with salt and pepper and 1 tablespoon of the chicken stock powder (or 1 beef stock cube).

Heat a large frying pan/skillet over a medium-high heat and add the olive oil. Brown the beef chunks on all sides, working in batches if you have a small pan. Each batch should be browned for about 5 minutes. Transfer the browned beef to a plate as you go.

Fry off half of the onions and garlic in the same pan over a low heat for about 5 minutes until soft.

COOK IT LOW & SLOW

Add the tomatoes, Scotch bonnet and the remaining onion and Romano peppers to a food processor or blender and blend until well mixed.

Pour this mixture into the casserole/Dutch oven or slow cooker pot and add the paprika, remaining chicken or beef stock, garlic powder, curry powder and thyme with 500 ml/2 cups water and add the browned beef cubes.

If you are using a lidded casserole/Dutch oven cook in a preheated oven at 165°C/325°F/Gas 3 for 2–4 hours. Check the meat after 2 hours; if it's not soft enough to shred with a fork, leave it for a further 1–2 hours. If you are using an electric slow cooker, cook on the low heat setting for 4–6 hours.

GET THE TACOS READY

While this is cooking, prepare the plantain tacos. Boil the prepared plantain until very soft. Drain and transfer to the food processor/blender, along with the salt and blend until smooth.

Put the flour and blended plantains in a bowl and knead until a dough forms.

Cut the dough into 6 medium chunks and roll each portion into a 15-cm/6-inch circle.

BRING IT ALL TOGETHER

Place each dough circle between two sheets of baking parchment and flatten with a taco press, rolling pin or the bottom of a pint glass. It doesn't matter which you use, just make sure the taco case can accommodate your beef and filling!

Heat the oil in a clean heavy-based frying pan/skillet and fry each taco for 2 minutes on each side over a medium heat until golden. Shape the tacos into pockets while still warm.

Once the beef is cooked, shred it into the sauce and assemble each taco with the beef filling and pile on the toppings. Don't worry if the plantain taco shells are cold you can reheat them in a pan or in the good old microwave if needed.

ASSEMBLE LIKE NIGERIA IN THE AFRICAN CUP OF NATIONS & ENJOY LIKE THE CHAMPION YOU ARE!

EGG ROLL

Nigerian egg roll is a popular small chop sold on the streets of Lagos, that can be eaten any time of day.

250 g/1¾ cups plain/all-purpose
   flour
50 g/¼ cup white granulated
   sugar
½ teaspoon baking powder
½ teaspoon salt
100 g/1 stick butter, melted
60 ml/¼ cup water
6 UK large/US extra-large eggs,
   soft-boiled and peeled
500 ml/2 cups vegetable oil,
   for deep frying

SEASONING
½ tablespoon paprika
½ tablespoon mixed herbs
½ tablespoon turmeric
½ tablespoon garlic powder
½ tablespoon mild curry powder

MAKES 6 EGG ROLLS

FIRST, MAKE THE DOUGH

In a large mixing bowl, combine the flour, sugar, baking powder and salt, along with the all the seasoning. Mix well to combine. Add the melted butter and mix until the mixture resembles coarse crumbs.

Gradually add water to the flour mixture, a little at a time, while mixing with your hands or a spoon. Continue adding water until a soft, slightly sticky dough forms. Knead the dough for a few minutes until it becomes smooth and elastic.

GET SHAPING

Divide the dough into 6 equal portions. Roll each portion into a ball.

Take one portion of the dough and flatten it into a circle on a clean and floured surface. Place a soft-boiled egg in the centre of the dough circle. Fold the dough over the egg, covering it completely and sealing the edges. Repeat this process for the remaining eggs and dough.

FRY IT UP

Heat the vegetable oil in a large saucepan or deep-fat fryer to about 180°C/350°F in temperature. Test the temperature of the oil by dropping a small piece of the dough in; if it floats, then the egg rolls are ready to fry.

Carefully place the wrapped eggs into the hot oil, a few at a time, depending on the size of your pan. Fry them until they are golden brown and crispy, turning occasionally to ensure even cooking. This should take about 6–8 minutes per batch.

Once the egg rolls are cooked and golden brown, remove them from the oil using a slotted spoon and drain them on paper towels to remove any excess oil.

Leave the egg rolls to cool slightly before chopping and serving.

EGGY NIGERIAN-STYLE OMELETTE

Eggy is our take on a Nigerian-style omelette, which is the perfect dish for breakfast or can be eaten with a late brunch. As you know, we Nigerians are all about abundance, so having a plain egg just isn't enough.

4 eggs, any size
vegetable oil, for shallow frying
½ a white onion, diced
4 chestnut/cremini mushrooms, diced
1 red Romano pepper, deseeded and diced
4 sun-dried tomatoes, sliced
100 g/2 cups baby leaf spinach
½ a Scotch bonnet chilli/chile, thinly sliced
1 teaspoon paprika
1 teaspoon dried mixed herbs
20 g/¾ oz grated Cheddar cheese (optional)
finely chopped spring onions/ scallions, to garnish (optional)
salt and freshly ground black pepper

SERVES 2 FLY PEOPLE

GET CRACKING

Crack and whisk the eggs in a mixing bowl, season with salt and pepper and set aside until needed.

Add some vegetable oil to a deep frying pan/skillet and set over a medium heat.

ADD SOME HEAT

Once the oil is hot, add the onion, mushrooms, Romano pepper, sun-dried tomatoes, spinach and Scotch bonnet to the pan and stir well.

Add the paprika and mixed herbs, season to taste with salt and pepper and stir well.

Fry for 2–3 minutes then add the whisked eggs and cheese, if using.

Cover the saucepan to allow the eggs to steam and rise. Cook for 6 minutes.

GET READY TO CHOP!

Garnish with finely chopped spring onions, if using, and serve.

ASUN TURKEY BITES

Asun is a Nigerian small chop typically made with smoked goat meat. Keeping to the nature of smoked meat, we adapted the Asun recipe by using smoked turkey wings that can be purchased from most Halal butchers. We would recommend asking the butcher to cut your wings into bite-sized pieces due to the dense bones.

2 kg/4½ lb. smoked turkey wings, cut into bite-sized pieces (ask the butcher to do this)
6 tablespoons vegetable oil
2 red Romano peppers, finely chopped
2–5 Scotch bonnet chillies/chiles (depending on how much heat you can handle), chopped
4 garlic cloves, crushed/minced
1 large red onion, chopped
1 tablespoon ground crayfish (optional)
salt

SEASONING
1 teaspoon fresh thyme
1 teaspoon ground cumin
1 tablespoon curry powder (we usually use hot)
1 teaspoon ground ginger
1 tablespoon garlic powder
2 tablespoons Jumbo chicken stock powder
1 teaspoon smoked paprika

TO SERVE
chopped fresh coriander/cilantro
mixed coloured (bell) peppers, sliced
dried chilli/chile flakes

SERVES 4 FLY PEOPLE

START WITH THE SEASONING
Preheat the oven to 220°C/425°F/Gas 7.

Mix all of the seasoning together in a small bowl and sprinkle over the turkey bites in a mixing bowl with 2 tablespoons of the vegetable oil. Use your hands to ensure the meat is evenly coated. Set aside in the fridge for 30 minutes, allowing the turkey bites to marinate.

Carefully place the seasoned turkey bites onto a baking sheet and bake for 30 minutes, turning halfway through the cooking time.

MAKE THE SWEET & SPICY SAUCE
Using a food processor, coarsely mince the Romano pepper, Scotch bonnets, garlic and red onion.

In a deep saucepan, heat the remaining 4 tablespoons of the vegetable oil and add the blended mixture and the crayfish, if using. Mix and cook for 5 minutes. Add salt to taste.

Once the turkey bites are cooked, combine the meat with the sauce in the saucepan and stir until the turkey bites are evenly coated with the sauce.

LET'S CHOP!
Garnish with fresh coriander, sliced peppers and chilli seeds.

5
SWEET
THINGS

PLANTAIN SOUFFLE PANCAKES

Light and fluffy, our Flygerian soufflé plantain pancakes. The ultimate crowd pleaser and a sensational twist on standard pancakes, the plantain adds another dimension to these airy delights and will send your palate wild. Trust us – this is another BANGER! This beautiful dish can be made vegan by using veggie oil and oat milk as an alternative. No one gets left behind at the Flygerians and these bad boys are delicious either way.

2 ripe plantains, peeled and cut into chunks

4 UK medium/US large eggs, separated

60 ml/¼ cup whole/full-fat milk (or dairy-free milk alternative)

1 teaspoon vanilla extract (optional)

1 tablespoon caster/superfine sugar (optional, or to taste)

60 g/½ cup plain/all-purpose flour

1 teaspoon baking powder

2 tablespoons butter or vegetable oil, plus extra for frying

salt

TOPPINGS

icing/confectioners' sugar

maple syrup or honey

100 g/¾ cup strawberries, cut in half

100 g/¾ cup blueberries

baking sheet lined with baking parchment

SERVES 4 FLY PEOPLE (2 MINI SOUFFLÉS EACH)

PREPARE YOURSELF FOR ENJOYMENT

Preheat the oven to 180°C/350°F/Gas 4.

Heat a drizzle of oil in a pan over a medium heat and fry the plantain until golden. Remove from the pan, leave to cool, then transfer to a blender or food processor.

Add the egg yolks, milk and vanilla extract, if using, to the blender with the plantains and blend until smooth and silky.

WHISK THESE BEAUTIFUL FLUFFY DREAMS

Grab a fresh mixing bowl, whisk together the sugar, flour, baking powder and a pinch of salt, then gently fold in the plantain mixture until it's well mixed together.

In another clean mixing bowl, beat the egg whites with a hand mixer or electric whisk until they stand in peak form.

Gently fold the egg whites into the plantain batter. When we say gently, we mean it – no heavy hands, we need the mixture standing taller than Big Ben! They may deflate slightly.

INCOMING HAPPINESS

Heat a non-stick frying pan/skillet or oven-safe pan over a medium heat and add a small amount of butter or oil to grease the surface. Once the pan has heated up, pour the plantain pancake batter into the pan. We like to make 2–4 pancakes at a time, but see what you can fit in your pan. Spread the batter evenly with a spatula and cook for 2 minutes on each side or until the edges set.

Transfer them to the lined baking sheet and bake in the oven for 8 minutes or until golden.

Carefully remove the soufflé plantain pancakes from the oven and serve straight away, while hot and steamy.

ADD YOUR CHOSEN TOPPINGS AND CHOP!

PLANTAIN WAFFLES

Plantain can take many forms and this one is a beautiful dish to set your day right. We make this banger when one of us has had a hard day. There is nothing like sisterly love and knowing you have someone in your corner, every step of the way on this journey we call life. We shared a room until we were 18 and moved into a house while we were both at university 30 minutes apart from each other. When the road gets tough, we will hold each other's hand every step of the way. This one we wanted to share with you to brighten your hard days or to just add some extra love to your day, because everyone needs a dish that warms their heart and puts a smile on their face.

2 ripe plantains, peeled and chopped
125 ml/½ cup whole/full-fat milk (or oat milk)
500 g/3¾ cups plain/all-purpose flour
2 teaspoons baking powder
1 teaspoon salt
2 UK large/US extra-large eggs
200 g/1 cup soft dark brown sugar (adjust to taste)
1 teaspoon vanilla extract
100 g/1 stick butter, melted, plus extra for greasing
icing/confectioners' sugar and maple syrup, to serve

waffle iron

**MAKES ABOUT
10 MEDIUM WAFFLES**

PURE JOY BEGINS HERE
Purée the chopped plantains with the milk in a blender until smooth.

In a large mixing bowl, combine the flour, baking powder and salt and mix well to combine.

In another bowl, whisk together the eggs, sugar, vanilla extract, melted butter and plantain purée until well combined.

LET'S GET IT COOKING
Preheat a waffle iron according to the manufacturer's instructions. Lightly grease the waffle iron to minimize burning.

Pour some of the batter onto the preheated waffle iron, using the recommended amount for your waffle iron size. Spread the batter evenly to cover the waffle grids.

Close the waffle iron and cook the waffles according to the manufacturer's instructions – typically for 3–5 minutes, or until the waffles are golden brown and crispy on the outside. Repeat until the batter has been used up, keeping the waffles warm as you cook.

CHOP LIFE (& THESE WAFFLES) BEFORE IT GETS COLD
Best served hot, dusted with icing sugar and maple syrup.

MILO RASPBERRY COOLIE CHEESECAKE

This cheesecake is a delicious and easy-to-make dessert that doesn't require baking in the oven, made using Milo chocolate malt powder. A simple recipe to impress your friends and family.

BASE

200 g/7 oz. Nigerian Chin Chin Biscuits (see page 128) or digestive biscuits/graham crackers

50 g/¼ cup white caster/superfine sugar

85 g/6 tablespoons unsalted butter, melted

FILLING

450 g/2 cups full-fat cream cheese, softened

240 ml/1 cup double/heavy cream, chilled

100 g/½ cup white caster/superfine sugar

1 teaspoon vanilla extract

50 g/½ cup Milo chocolate malt powder

TOPPING

125 g/1 cup fresh raspberries

50 g/⅓ cup white icing/confectioners' sugar, plus extra for dusting

a few strawberries, hulled and sliced

Milo chocolate malt powder, for dusting

a 23-cm/9-inch pie tin or pie dish

SERVES 4-6 FLY PEOPLE

FIRST, MAKE THE CHEESECAKE BASE

In a mixing bowl, combine the Chin Chin biscuits/cookies, sugar and melted butter. Mix until the butter combines with the crushed biscuits. Press the mixture firmly into the bottom of the pie tin or pie dish, spreading evenly. Use the bottom of a glass to press the base firmly and pop in the freezer for 20 minutes while you prepare the filling.

MAKE IT SMOOTH & CREAMY

Grab a large mixing bowl. Use an electric whisk or balloon whisk and beat the softened cream cheese until smooth.

Grab another clean bowl and whip the cream until it forms stiff peaks.

Slowly add the sugar to the cream cheese and beat until it's all combined. Add the vanilla extract and Milo and mix until smooth.

Gently fold the cream into the cream cheese mixture until combined. Gently does it – you don't want to deflate the whipped cream.

OUR DEAR FLYGERIAN RECRUIT, IT'S TIME TO ASSEMBLE YOUR BEAUTIFUL CHEESECAKE

Get your base out of the freezer and pour the filling on top of the biscuit base, using a spatula to spread it evenly.

Cover the cheesecake with foil and refrigerate for 3–4 hours, or overnight, because you can never have too much setting time.

Crush 100 g/¾ cup of the raspberries, place in a small saucepan with the icing sugar and 100 ml/scant ½ cup water. Cook for 10 minutes and set aside to cool down to room temperature. You've just made your raspberry coolie.

MAKE IT LOOK SEXY & SERVE!

Grab the gorgeously set Milo cheesecake, top with the raspberry coolie and arrange some sliced strawberries and extra raspberries on top. Dust with Milo and icing sugar.

PUFF PUFF
NIGERIAN DOUGHNUTS

Puff Puff is one of the most famous, tasty, tantalizing dishes in Nigeria, sold by street vendors on stalls or people carrying them in snack bags. This perfect dessert and sharing sweet treat is Nigeria's answer to a doughnut. Our grandma made the best puff puffs – beautifully handcrafted and crunchy on the outside and sweet and delicious on the inside. Whenever she heard we were coming over, she would make a big batch of batter, leaving it to ferment for a short period of time to achieve its fluffy centre. This is what sets hers apart and left us wanting more. She would serve them warm and we would fill her in on our week and we would laugh while tucking in, and she'd always be frying more to fill us up before we set off back home. These delights will always have a special place in our hearts.

2 tablespoons dried yeast
1 tablespoon vanilla extract
500 ml/2 cups lukewarm water
500 g/3¾ cups plain/all-purpose flour
150 g/¾ cup white granulated sugar
1 teaspoon ground cinnamon
1 teaspoon ground nutmeg
1 litre/4 cups vegetable oil, for deep frying
icing/confectioners' sugar and Milo chocolate malt powder, to sprinkle (optional)
salt

MAKES 15-20
LARGE PUFF PUFFS

GOODNESS STARTS HERE

Mix the yeast and vanilla extract into the lukewarm water and leave to sit for 5 minutes for the yeast to activate.

Meanwhile, sift the flour into a large bowl and add the sugar, cinnamon, nutmeg and a pinch of salt.

Mix the yeast water into the flour bowl and stir until the batter is of a smooth and sticky consistency. If the batter is too thick, add more lukewarm water.

Cover the batter with cling film/plastic wrap and leave to rest for 1 hour. After an hour the mixture should have fermented, ensuring a fluffy fry.

IT'S GETTING HOT IN HERE

Heat the vegetable oil in a deep saucepan or a deep-fat fryer to about 180°C/350°F. You will know the oil is ready by dropping a small piece of the batter into the oil. If it rises, then the puff puff is ready to fry.

THIS WILL CHANGE YOUR LIFE

Using an ice cream scoop, scoop the mixture and carefully place it in the hot oil. Cook over a medium heat, ensuring the individual puffs do not stick together, until the puff puffs are a golden colour all over. It roughly takes 2–3 minutes to fry the first batch of puffs. Transfer to paper towels to drain any excess oil once cooked.

Sprinkle the puffs with icing sugar and Milo, if liked.

CHIN CHIN
NIGERIAN BISCUITS

Nigerian Chin Chin is a popular crunchy snack made from a simple dough that's fried until golden brown. It's like a biscuit/cookie, that can be enjoyed any time of the day. Be warned though – once you start chopping, it's hard to stop. It's commonly enjoyed as a snack but can be used as a dessert or an appetizer while you wait for your food.

500 g/3¾ cups plain/all-purpose flour
100 g/½ cup white granulated sugar
½ teaspoon baking powder
¼ teaspoon salt
½ teaspoon ground nutmeg
¼ teaspoon ground cinnamon (optional)
100 g/1 stick butter, melted
2 UK large/US extra-large eggs
60–80 ml/¼–⅓ cup evaporated milk or water (or as needed)
vegetable oil, for frying

SERVES ANYTHING FROM 2 TO 10 AS A LIGHT SNACK

START MIXING
In a large mixing bowl, sift together the flour, sugar, baking powder, salt, nutmeg and cinnamon, if using.

Make a well in the centre of the dry ingredients and add the melted butter and eggs. Mix the ingredients together using a wooden spoon or your hands until a crumbly dough forms.

Gradually add the evaporated milk or water, a little at a time, while kneading the dough until it comes together into a smooth, firm dough. Be careful not to add too much liquid, as the dough should be firm and not sticky.

START SHAPING
Divide the dough into smaller portions and roll each portion out on a floured surface to about 5 mm/¼ inch thickness.

Use a knife or pizza cutter to cut the rolled-out dough into small rectangles or diamond shapes, about 2.5 cm/1 inch long.

LET'S GET IT COOKING
Heat the vegetable oil in a deep-frying pan or pot over medium heat until around 180°C/350°F. To test if the oil is hot enough for frying, drop in a small piece of dough. If it sizzles and browns immediately, it's ready to go.

Carefully add the cut pieces of dough to the hot oil in batches, making sure not to overcrowd the pan. Fry for 3–5 minutes, or until they are golden brown and crispy, turning them occasionally for even frying.

Once cooked, transfer to paper towels to remove any excess oil. Allow the Chin Chin to cool completely before serving.

Store the cooled Chin Chin in an airtight container at room temperature for up to several weeks.

CHIN CHIN CRUMBLE

Another sensational twist on an outstanding, simple, classic British dessert. Chin Chin is a sweet Nigerian biscuit/cookie that you can find throughout Nigeria and in neighbouring countries. This elite street food staple has a grab-and-go nature and is delicious with a cuppa to satisfy your sugar cravings. Combined with the sharp sweet taste of apple, this dessert is perfect with fresh vanilla custard or clotted/heavy cream.

2 kg/4½ lb. plain Chin Chin biscuits/cookies, crushed (see page 128 or buy ready-made)

8 ripe green apples (Granny Smith is our preference), peeled and sliced

125 g/scant ¾ cup soft dark brown sugar

1 teaspoon ground cinnamon

1 teaspoon vanilla extract

1 tablespoon fresh lemon juice

1 tablespoon honey

1 tablespoon cornflour/ cornstarch

1 tablespoon ground nutmeg

100 g/1 stick unsalted butter, melted

custard or clotted/heavy cream, to serve

46 x 33 cm/18 x 13 inch baking dish

SERVES 4-6 FLY PEOPLE

LET'S GET STARTED
Preheat the oven to 180°C/350°F/Gas 4.

Place the Chin Chin in batches in a food processor and pulse until it is broken down into a crumble texture. Repeat the process until all the Chin Chin have been crumbled.

Place the sliced apples, brown sugar, cinnamon, vanilla extract, lemon juice, honey, cornflour and nutmeg in a saucepan. Stir well, ensuring the apples are evenly coated with all the flavours. Cook over a medium heat for 10 minutes to allow the apples to slightly soften.

Transfer the apple mixture to the baking dish.

BUILD THE MAGIC
In large mixing bowl, place the crumbled Chin Chin and mix in the melted butter so that the biscuits are infused with the butter.

Evenly spread the Chin Chin mixture on top of the apples, until the apples are completely covered.

Bake for 20–30 minutes until golden and crisp on top. Leave to cool slightly before serving.

LET'S CHOP!
Best served hot and with custard or cream.

NAIJA FRENCH TOAST

In Nigeria we don't usually eat dessert, we have an ethos 'if you feed me right the first and second time, then there's no need for a third'. As you dive through this book, you will discover a few recipes have been created and inspired by our dual nationalities. Nigeria has our heart, but London is home.

2 UK large/US extra-large eggs
125 ml/½ cup whole/full-fat milk
    (or oat milk)
1 teaspoon vanilla extract
2 tablespoons Lotus Biscoff
    Topping Sauce, plus extra
    to drizzle
½ teaspoon ground cinnamon
    (optional)
½ tablespoon ground nutmeg
2 teaspoons unsalted butter
4 slices thickly cut Agege Bread
    (see page 23)

TO SERVE
vanilla ice cream
100 g/3½ oz. Lotus Biscoff
    biscuits/cookies, crumbled
icing/confectioners' sugar,
    for dusting
fresh fruit of your choice
    (optional)

SERVES 2 FLY PEOPLE

HIT IT WITH THE WHISK
Whisk the eggs, milk, vanilla extract, Biscoff sauce, cinnamon, if using, and nutmeg in a shallow bow until everything is thoroughly mixed.

Add the butter to a frying pan/skillet and heat over a medium heat.

LET'S GET THEM WET
Submerge the agege bread slices into the egg mixture, ensuring each side is coated evenly.

Transfer the coated agege bread slices to the hot frying pan and cook for about 2 minutes on each side until golden brown.

TIME FOR ANOTHER BANGER
When cooked, transfer to a plate and continue with the remaining bread slices, adding extra butter to the pan as needed.

Serve the Naija French toast warm with vanilla ice cream, a drizzle of Biscoff spread, crumbled Biscoff biscuits, a dusting of icing sugar and fresh fruit of your choice, if liked.

CHIN'OFFEE PIE

A Flygerians' original, created as a sweet treat for our grandma who loved banoffee pie – a British staple. We wanted to fuse together our dual nationality and create a dish that showcased the best of both countries in all its glory.

3 ripe bananas, sliced
aerated 'squirty' canned cream
Nigerian Milo chocolate malt
powder, cocoa powder or
grated chocolate, for dusting
(optional)

CRUST
1kg/2¼ lb. Chin Chin biscuits
(see page 128), crushed
100 g/1 stick unsalted butter

CARAMEL FILLING
100 g/1 stick unsalted butter
400 g/14 oz. sweetened
condensed milk

a 23-cm/9-inch cake tin

SERVES 4-8 FLY PEOPLE

LET THE LEGENDARY DISH BEGIN

First prepare the crust. Crush the Chin Chin biscuits into fine crumbs so the base comes out smooth. You can use a blender or place the biscuits in a sealed plastic bag and crush them with a rolling pin.

Melt the butter and mix it with the crushed biscuits until it forms a well combined mixture.

Press the mixture firmly into the bottom of the cake tin, spreading evenly. Use the bottom of a glass to press the base firmly. Pop the base into the fridge for 1 hour while you prepare the filling.

GET THE FILLING TOGETHER

Make the caramel filling by melting the butter in a saucepan over a medium heat. Add the condensed milk and stir continuously until it starts to thicken – this may take 10–15 minutes and should be a lovely golden, heavy, thick texture.

Pop the caramel in the fridge to chill for 15 minutes. Remove from the fridge and spread the caramel over the Chin Chin crust. Return the tin to the fridge for at least 2 hours to set.

COMBINE GREATNESS

Top the chilled pie with the sliced bananas and cover the whole surface of the pie with canned squirty cream. Dust with Milo, cocoa powder or grated chocolate, if liked, to finish.

ENJOYMENT TIME!

NOTES

» To make the pie last longer, only add bananas and whipped cream once each portion has been individually sliced. If you plan on serving the whole pie that day, then follow the above method.

» If you don't feel like making your own caramel, shop bought will do.

AGEGE BREAD & BUTTER PUDDING

A Nigerian twist on a British classic. Think bread and butter pudding but better!

1 loaf of Agege Bread (see page 23), cut into 8 slices
butter, for greasing
500 ml/2 cups oat milk
150 g/¾ cup soft dark brown sugar
2 UK large/US extra-large eggs
1 teaspoon vanilla extract
1 tablespoon ground cinnamon

1 tablespoon ground nutmeg
salt

FILLING
200 g/1½ cups mixed dried fruits, chopped (raisins, raspberries, cranberries)
100 g/⅔ cup white chocolate chips

SERVES 4-6 FLY PEOPLE

CAN YOU FEEL THE HEAT?
Preheat the oven to 180°C/350°F/Gas 4. Grease a deep ovenproof baking dish with butter.

Spread the slices of agege bread with butter on each side. Place the buttered bread slices in the greased dish, allowing the bread to overlap.

BRING IT ALL TOGETHER
Warm the oat milk in the microwave for 1 minute.

In a separate bowl, whisk together the sugar, eggs, vanilla extract, cinnamon, nutmeg and a pinch of salt. Slowly pour the warm milk into the egg mixture, whisking constantly to combine.

Spread the whisked egg mixture over the bread, ensuring it is evenly covered and leave to soak for 15 minutes.

Sprinkle the dried fruit and white chocolate chips over the top. Bake for 30 minutes until golden brown on top.

TIP Drizzle with icing/confectioners' sugar for extra sweetness and serve with your favourite ice cream or custard, if liked.

LAGOS MESS

This is really a Flygerian special right here, inspired by the British Eton mess. It's a simple yet delicious dessert traditionally made with a combination of whipped cream, crushed meringue and fresh berries. We made this as a dessert for our family in Lagos and they loved it, hence the name. It is beautiful chaos on a plate, just like the streets of Lagos.

240 ml/1 cup double/heavy cream
2 tablespoons white granulated sugar
100 ml/scant ½ cup Courvoisier
6 meringue nests or about 1 cup of store-bought meringue cookies, crushed

500 g/3⅓ cups fresh strawberries, hulled and sliced (or other berries of your choice)
220 g/1 cup Chin Chin biscuits/cookies, crushed (see page 128 or buy ready-made)

SERVES 3-6 FLY PEOPLE

TIME TO MIX THE MAGIC
In a large mixing bowl, whip the cream with the sugar until stiff peaks form. Slowly pour in the Courvoisier and mix to combine.

Gently fold the crushed meringue or cookies into the cream, being careful not to deflate the mixture.

Reserve a few sliced strawberries for garnish and fold the remaining strawberries into the cream.

LAYER IT UP
Spoon the mixture into serving glasses or bowls, layering it with additional strawberries if desired.

Garnish each serving with a few strawberry slices and crushed Chin Chin. Serve immediately.

SPREAD THE LOVE

SUGARCANE CASH COOKIES

These sugarcane cookies are perfect for enjoying with a cup of tea or coffee, or as a sweet snack any time of day. Store any leftovers in an airtight container for freshness.

120 g/1 stick unsalted butter, softened

100 g/½ cup white granulated sugar, plus extra for rolling

100 ml/scant ½ cup sugarcane juice (or sugarcane syrup or sugar syrup)

1 UK large/US extra-large egg

120g /½ cup mixed peanuts and cashew nuts

1 teaspoon vanilla extract

260 g/2 cups plain/all-purpose flour

½ teaspoon baking powder
 teaspoon salt

a baking sheet, lined with baking parchment or lightly greased

MAKES 8-10 COOKIES

LET'S GET THESE BEAUTIES IN MOTION
Preheat the oven to 175°C/350°F/Gas 4.

In a large mixing bowl, cream together the softened butter and sugar until light and fluffy.

Add the sugarcane juice (or syrup), egg, mixed peanuts and cashew nuts and vanilla extract to the bowl and mix well.

MIX THINGS UP
Grab a separate bowl, mix together the flour, baking powder and salt until combined.

Gradually add the dry ingredients to the wet ingredients, mixing until a dough forms. If the dough is too sticky, you can add a little more flour.

TIME TO CUT SOME SHAPES
Shape the cookie dough into small balls, about 2 cm/1 inch in diameter. If desired, roll each ball in sugar for a sparkling finish.

Place the cookie dough balls onto the prepared baking sheet, leaving some space between each cookie. Use the bottom of a glass or the palm of your hand to gently flatten each cookie slightly.

GIVE IT TO DEM!
Bake the cookies in the preheated oven for 10–12 minutes, or until the edges are golden brown.

Remove the cookies from the oven and let them cool on the baking sheet for a few minutes before transferring them to a wire rack to cool completely. Once cooled, serve the sugarcane cookies and enjoy their delicious flavour.

PLANTAIN & BAILEY'S ICE CREAM

Name a better underrated duo! Our Mum would make this to mark a special occasion or to just brighten our days after school (without the Baileys of course!). It has always been a go-to dessert, that's bound to cool the palate and warm the soul. We added Baileys into the mix as it was our Mum's and late Grandma's (also known as Mama's) favourite drink at Christmas. This dish is great with Puff Puff (see page 127).

2 ripe plantains (the blacker the dots, the better the taste – you want the plantain to be soft and sweet)

100 ml/scant ½ cup vegetable oil

125 ml/½ cup whole/full-fat milk

500 ml /2 cups double/heavy cream

125 ml/½ cup Baileys, or other Irish cream liqueur

4 UK large/US extra-large egg yolks

50 ml/3½ tablespoons runny honey

2 teaspoons vanilla extract

a pinch of ground nutmeg

salt

TO SERVE (OPTIONAL)

ice cream cones

Fried Plantain (see page 103)

Chin Chin Nigerian Biscuits (see page 128), crumbled

ice cream maker (optional)

SERVES 4-8 FLY PEOPLE

(DEPENDING ON HOW MUCH DELICIOUSNESS YOUR BELLY CAN HANDLE)

TIP To make this non-alcoholic, replace the Baileys with the same volume in milk.

FIRST, FRY & PURÉE THE PLANTAIN

Peel the skin off the plantains and chop the flesh into chunks. Fry the plantain in the vegetable oil in a frying pan/skillet over a low heat for about 4 minutes on each side until golden.

Transfer the fried plantain to a food processor or blender, add 100 ml/ scant ½ cup water and pulse until smooth.

Put the puréed plantains, milk, cream and Baileys in a saucepan and cook over a medium heat for about 10 minutes until it starts to steam. Don't allow the mixture to boil. Take off the heat.

CREATE THE ICE-CREAM BASE

Beat the egg yolks and honey in a bowl until the mixture is combined and thickened.

Slowly pour the plantain mixture into the egg yolk mixture, whisking continuously to temper the egg.

Transfer the mixture back to the pan and simmer over a low heat, stirring all the time, until it slightly thickens and coats the back of a spoon. This should take 10–20 minutes, but make sure it doesn't boil.

WE ARE ALMOST THERE, GO YOU!

Remove the mixture from the heat, stir in the vanilla extract, nutmeg and a pinch of salt.

Strain the mixture through a fine-mesh sieve/strainer – no one likes lumpy ice cream do they? Let that bad boy cool down to room temperature, then cover and refrigerate for at least 1 hour.

Pop it in an ice cream maker and churn according to the manufacturer's instructions to a soft consistency.

NO ICE CREAM MAKER, NO PROBLEM

Add your mixture to a sandwich bag and freeze for 4 hours. Once frozen, pop it back in the food processor or blender until it fluffs out into an ice cream texture.

6
DRINKS

MR CHAPS

Our take on a famous Nigerian welcome drink that was made by a Lagos barman who wanted to create a drink for an English gentlemen called Mr Chapman that embodied Nigeria's bittersweet beauty. This is Chapmans Flygerians' style! Chapman should be sweet like sunset and bursting with fruity flavour. The longer you leave the cucumber in, the stronger its flavour. Play around with the ingredients until you find the sweetness balance that makes your palate dance and enjoy!

2 cups ice cubes

2 fresh oranges

2 fresh lemons

1 litre/4 cups carbonated water/ soda

100 ml/scant ½ cup sugarcane syrup

50 ml/3½ tablespoons grenadine syrup

12 dashes of Angostura bitters

4 blood orange or orange slices

6 lime slices

6 lemon slices

4 cucumber slices

200 ml/scant 1 cup of your favourite non-flavoured vodka

a 500-ml/2-cup capacity jug/ pitcher

SERVES 4-6 AUTHENTIC FLYGERIANS CHAPMANS

LET'S START

Fill the jug with the ice cubes.

Freshly squeeze and pour in the juice from the oranges and lemons.

ADD SOME FIZZ

Add half the carbonated water – you can add the rest at the end depending on how strong you'd like it; we love it to have a kick.

Add the sugarcane syrup, grenadine syrup and the Angostura bitters. Add the sliced fruits, cucumber and the vodka.

Stir the mixture with the power of your ancestors to blend all the ingredients.

SIT BACK & LET THE BEAUTIFUL TASTE TAKE YOU ON

Serve the Flygerians' Chapman in glasses filled with ice.

CUCUMBER MARGARITA

A light, refreshing drink perfect for summer!

⅓ cucumber, peeled
220 ml/scant 1 cup
   silver tequila
120 ml/½ cup triple
   sec or Cointreau
120 ml/½ cup fresh
   lime juice
60 ml/¼ cup agave
   syrup
ice cubes

TO GARNISH
1 lime wedge
50 g/¼ cup pink
   Himalayan finely

crushed salt,
   or normal salt
50 g/¼ cup
   pomegranate seeds
long cucumber
   shavings (made
   using a potato
   peeler)
4 lime wheels
   (optional)

cocktail sticks/
toothpicks

SERVES 4 FLY PEOPLE

FIRST, RIM THE GLASSES
Rim 4 rocks/tumbler glasses with pink salt by running a lime wedge around the rim of the glasses, then dipping the rim into the salt. Set aside.

START MAKING YOUR MARGARITA
Blend the cucumber in a blender or juicer to release the juices. Half fill a cocktail shaker with ice and add the blended cucumber, tequila, Cointreau, lime juice and agave syrup.

THROW ON SOME TIWA SAVAGE ('KOROBA')
Shake the cocktail shaker for about 20 seconds. Fill the salt-rimmed glasses to the top with ice and evenly strain the mixture into the glasses. Add some pomegranate seeds to each glass.

FINISH WITH A FLOURISH
Add a lime wheel to the rim of the glasses, if liked. Curl the cucumber shavings and pin with a cocktail stick to hold together and pop one into each glass!

BOOM!

KIWI STRAWBERRY CRUSH

This is a beautiful, refreshing cocktail, perfect as an all-year-round pleaser.

6 kiwis, peeled and
   finely sliced (reserve
   some to garnish)
12 strawberries, hulled
   (6 to crush and
   reserve 6 to slice for
   garnish)
300 ml/1¼ cups white
   rum (we like to use
   Wray & Nephew
   Overproof Rum)
150 ml/⅔ cup fresh
   lime juice

150 ml/⅔ cup
   sugarcane syrup
500 ml/2 cups chilled
   carbonated
   strawberry water
   (such as Radnor
   or Rubicon)
crushed ice, to shake
   and serve

SERVES 6 FLY PEOPLE

(OR 2 PEOPLE
LOOKING TO HAVE
A GREAT TIME!)

FIRST UP, MUDDLE SOME FLAVOUR INTENSITY!
Crush the kiwi slices and 6 strawberries in a bowl until puréed. You can use a small blender or food processor if you prefer.

Use the remaining fruit slices to line 6 highball glasses and fill them with crushed ice. Set aside until needed.

GET SHAKING
Fill a cocktail shaker with crushed ice. Add the puréed fruit, rum, lime juice and sugarcane syrup to the shaker.

PLAY SKALES, 'SHAKE BODY', AND DO AS THE SONG SAYS...
Distribute the mixture in your shaker evenly between the ice-filled glasses. Top up with carbonated strawberry water.

DRINK AND DANCE LIKE NO ONE'S WATCHING!

'GIVE IT TO DEM' CHILLI LYCHEE MARGARITA

'Give it to dem' is a popular Nigerian Pigeon English phrase meaning to demonstrate one's power, charismatic ability and party hard nature. It's a phrase that embodies what it means to be Fly – you can often hear when someone is moving with excellence.

1 lime

2 tablespoons each crushed dried chilli/hot red pepper flakes and pink Himalayan salt, mixed together

120 ml/½ cup tequila (we love Don Julio but any tequila of your choosing will work wonders)

80 ml/⅓ cup triple sec or Cointreau

80 ml/⅓ cup lychee juice

60 ml/¼ cup fresh lime juice

60 ml/¼ cup agave syrup

4 whole lychees, peeled and deseeded, to garnish

ice cubes, to serve

SERVES 4 FLY PEOPLE

GRAB YOUR FAVOURITE GLASSES
Rim 4 chilled cocktail glasses by running a lime wedge around the rim of the glasses, then dipping the rim into the crushed chillies and pink salt mixture.

SHAKE WHAT YOUR MAMA GAVE YOU TO YOUR FAVOURITE AFROBEATS BANGER
Place all the liquid ingredients into a cocktail shaker half filled with ice and get shaking.

Add ice to the rimmed glasses and divide your cocktail evenly between them. Garnish with lychees.

ENJOYMENT IS YOURS
Whether you're gearing up to party or having a chilled one with friends, kick back and sip this tequila delight.

ZOBO DREAMS

The Emperor, the conqueror, the champion, the Lion is here! This is the only way to describe this nutritious, yet delicious Nigerian staple. Made from hibiscus leaves, this drink is enjoyed across West Africa and beyond, with the option to add alcohol for an extra kickstart. It has so many benefits including being rich in antioxidants and vitamin C. Its rich, vibrant appearance also has amazing properties like aiding digestion and supporting overall wellbeing so, if anything, this is a zobo dream of joy and goodness. We love fizzy zobo as there is noting more satisfying to quench that thirst.

440 g/1 lb. hibiscus (zobo) leaves, fresh or dried
200 g/1 cup granulated white sugar or 200 ml/scant 1 cup sugarcane syrup
1 tablespoon grated fresh ginger (adjust quantity to taste)
6 cloves
1 teaspoon dried chilli/hot red pepper flakes (optional)
240 ml/1 cup fresh pineapple juice
240 ml/1 cup fresh orange juice
1 litre/4 cups carbonated water/soda
300 ml/1¼ cups vodka (optional)
1 small cucumber, sliced (no need to peel)
1 large orange, sliced
1 large lemon, sliced

juicer (optional)
fine-mesh sieve/strainer or muslin/cheesecloth

SERVES 4–6 FLY PEOPLE

GRAB THE HIBISCUS LEAVES
Submerge them in a bowl of warm water for 15 minutes to get rid of any dust or sand.

Rinse the hibiscus leaves and place them in a saucepan with 500 ml/2 cups water and bring to the boil over a medium heat – this should take about 20 minutes. Reduce the heat to low and let it simmer for 10 minutes. Remove from the stove and let that bad boy cool down at room temperature.

Pour the hibiscus leaves through a fine-mesh sieve or muslin into a bowl to strain. Remove and discard the leaves and transfer the liquid to a clean container.

SUGAR TIME!
Add the sugar or sugarcane syrup to the hibiscus liquid and give it a stir until the sugar is completely dissolved. (If you are using sugarcane syrup still stir.) Add more to make it sweeter, if liked.

Add the ginger, cloves, dried chilli flakes, if using, and pineapple and orange juices to the mixture. Stir for a few minutes.

BRING IT ALL TOGETHER
Add ice cubes, the sweetened hibiscus water, carbonated water and vodka, if using, to a large jug/pitcher and add the cucumber, orange and lemon slices.

ENJOY!
Divide between serving glasses.

NOTE It's better to use freshly squeezed juices, but if you can't, juice from a carton is okay, too.

SUPERMALT MARTINI

This is one of our daring recipes, which may turn faces but trust us, this drink 'SLAPS'. When we say chop life, we mean it to the fullest! There is not one drink that can't be turned into an alcoholic cocktail, but if you don't like supermalt, skip to the next recipe. If you want to impress your guests with something different, get mixing this bittersweet cocktail shaken over ice.

ice cubes
160 ml/⅔ cup Supermalt
45 ml/1½ oz. dry vermouth
90 ml/⅓ cup vodka or gin
olive, to garnish (optional)

SERVES 3 FLY PEOPLE

START WITH THE ICE
Fill a cocktail shaker with ice cubes.

Pour in the Supermalt, dry vermouth and vodka (we prefer vodka) or gin.

GRAB YOUR SPEAKER & SHAKE WHAT YOUR MAMA GAVE YOU TO WIZKID 'DON'T DULL'
Shake the cocktail shaker vigorously for about 15–20 seconds to chill the ingredients and properly mix them.

Pour the mixture into 3 chilled martini glasses. Garnish with an olive or 3, if you want to keep that classic feel.

ENJOY!

LAGOS RISE & SHINE

Lagos – where money doesn't sleep, nor do the people. Rumour has it that tequila will boost your mood – we certainly feel great after drinking it. Trying this recipe with a dash of your favourite cognac is certified to take the edge off the day.

100 ml/scant ½ cup tequila
200 ml/scant 1 cup Cognac (we use Courvoisier)
360 ml/1½ cups blood orange juice or orange juice (freshly squeezed preferably)
60 ml/¼ cup grenadine syrup

TO SERVE
ice cubes
orange slices or blood orange slices, to decorate

SERVES 4 FLY PEOPLE

GET STARTED
Fill 4 tall glasses with ice cubes.

Pour the tequila over the ice in each glass (25 ml/1 oz. per glass).

CREATE SOME LAYERS
Slowly pour the blood orange juice into the glasses, allowing it to settle at the bottom.

Pour the grenadine syrup over the back of a spoon or the side of each glass, allowing it to sink to the bottom and create a layered effect.

DECORATE TO FINISH
Decorate each glass with an orange slice and there you have it, a welcoming drink. Serve immediately.

PARTY NO DE STOP COCKTAIL

A popular cocktail featuring Courvoisier cognac is the classic 'Sidecar'. Here's our Flygerian tequila version, that's bound to keep you dancing like no one's watching. We believe in being your most authentic self and living freely. When we say raise a toast to celebrate your very existence, this is the drink you need in your hand, because there is truly no one like you.

240 ml/1 cup white tequila (we love Don Julio)
120 ml/½ cup triple sec or Cointreau
100 ml/scant ½ cup freshly squeezed lemon juice

TO SERVE
½ lemon
sugar, for rimming
ice cubes
lemon twists

SERVES 4 FLY PEOPLE

RIM THE GLASSES
Rim 4 chilled cocktail glasses with sugar by running a lemon wedge around the rim of the glasses, then dipping the rim into sugar.

Fill a cocktail shaker with ice cubes.

Add the tequila, triple sec or Cointreau and freshly squeezed lemon juice to the shaker.

YOU KNOW WHAT TIME IT IS! PLAY OMAH LAY 'HOLY GHOST' & SHAKE YOUR BODY WITH THE COCKTAIL SHAKER IN HAND
Strain the mixture into the prepared cocktail glasses.

Garnish with a lemon twist.

SIP THIS BADDIE & ENJOY!

NAIJA GUINNESS PUNCH

Guinness punch is a party must have! A drink originating from our beautiful Caribbean family. Growing up with our Jamaican side of the family it was a must have at family barbecues and Christmas, and treated as a dessert post meal. With each sip we can still smell the richness of the Guinness that filled the room, still hear the laughter from our Dad and uncles that followed and the sound of dominos being slapped on the table, while our brother and cousins fought over who had the control pad for the next FIFA match.

500 ml/2 cups sweetened
 condensed milk
250 ml/1 cup evaporated milk
250 ml/1 cup single/light cream
 (Flygerian twist)
500 g/2½ cups white granulated
 sugar (adjust to taste)
200 ml/scant 1 cup white rum
 (we like to use Wray & Nephew
 Overproof Rum)
1.2 litres/5 cups Nigerian
 Guinness stout (we
 recommend using the bottles
 for the real stout taste)
2 tablespoons ground sweet
 cinnamon
2 tablespoons ground nutmeg,
 plus extra to garnish
2 tablespoons vanilla extract
ice cubes, to serve
long cinnamon sticks and
 physallis/cape gooseberries,
 to garnish

*a large jug/pitcher or punch
 bowl*

SERVES 6-8 FLY PEOPLE!

LET'S GO!

Grab a large punch bowl or jug/pitcher, combine the wonderful sweetened condensed milk, evaporated milk, cream and granulated sugar. Turn with a spoon until the mixture is well combined. Add the rum and give it a stir.

ADD SOME DEPTH

Gently pour the Guinness into the punch bowl or jug, add the cinnamon, nutmeg and vanilla extract and stir until all the ingredients are mixed in well.

Taste the beautiful creamy punch and add more sugar If needed. Fill glasses with ice cubes, ladle or pour in the punch, dust with ground nutmeg and add a cinnamon stick stirrer to each glass.

**DANCE ON THE TABLE
WITH A GLASS! CHEERS!**

PLANTAIN COLADA

A Flygerians' original. 'If you like pina coladas and getting caught in the rain...' this will transform your life. The perfect combo of creamy, refreshing sweetness and palate-cleansing, makes it a great cocktail to be enjoyed alone or with guests.

1 plantain, peeled, sliced and fried in vegetable oil or without oil in an air fryer

1 ripe yellow banana, peeled

250 g/1 cup crushed ice

120 ml/½ cup white rum (we like to use Wray & Nephew Overproof Rum)

300 ml/1¼ cups freshly blended pineapple juice (or shop-brought pineapple juice)

200 ml/scant 1 cup coconut milk (or coconut cream or 100 ml /scant ½ cup coconut rum)

100 ml/scant ½ cup fresh lime juice

4 drops of vanilla extract

100 ml/scant ½ cup agave syrup or runny honey

ice cubes, to serve

fresh lime slices, to garnish

SERVES 4-6 FLY PEOPLE

LET'S BLEND

Blend together the fried plantain, banana, ice, rum, pineapple juice, coconut milk, lime juice, vanilla extract and agave or honey.

Strain the mixture through a sieve/strainer.

COMBINE GREATNESS

Grab your glasses, add two cubes of ice per glass, pour, garnish with a slice of lime and enjoy.

GINGER ME IMMUNE BOOSTER

There are many colloquial terms for ginger in Nigeria... but when we say 'Ginger Me', we mean cleanse our mind, body and soul. Packed with antioxidants, this is the perfect drink to give you a boost during winter! Best served chilled.

1 kg/2¼ lb. fresh pineapple, peeled and cut into chunks

250 g/9 oz. fresh ginger root, peeled and chopped

1 tablespoon ground cinnamon

2 tablespoons fresh lime juice

250 g/1¼ cups granulated sugar (adjust to taste)

TO SERVE
ice cubes
fresh mint leaves (optional)
1 lime slice

MAKES 1 LITRE/ 4 CUPS JUICE

BLEND IT UP

Place the chopped pineapple and ginger in a blender in batches, adding a little water to loosen as you blend to a smooth consistency.

Pour the blended pineapple and ginger mixture through a fine-mesh sieve/strainer into a large bowl. Squeeze the mixture to extract as much juice as possible.

ADD SOME HEAT

Place the strained mixture into a large saucepan and add 1 litre/4 cups water, as well as the cinnamon, lime juice and sugar. Bring to the boil, then lower the heat and simmer over a low heat for about 15 minutes to allow the flavours to meld together. Stir occasionally.

Allow the mixture to cool as it is best served chilled over ice and garnished with mint leaves, if using, and lime slices.

PAW PAW
PALM WINE

The backbone of our alcoholic beverage community, palm wine popularly known as 'emu' or 'nkwu' in the Nigerian Igbo language or 'ode' in Yoruba, is a beverage associated with traditional ceremonies, festivals and all of the finest social gatherings. We will never forget the walks with our beautiful father (who made sure we were enriched with our culture despite being born in London) to a small Nigerian shop near Dalston Market to pick up some palm wine for our guests. He would talk us through how it was made from the sap of palm trees, part of the rich agriculture of Nigeria. Go to any market in Nigeria and you are bound to see an aunty or uncle selling sweet yet sour palm wine to wet your whistle on a warm summer's day. This drink is inspired by the vibrancy and beauty of our heritage and our British love for Prosecco (did you know the largest market for Prosecco is in the UK?).

2 large ripe and juicy paw paw
  (papaya)
200 ml/scant 1 cup sugarcane
  syrup or runny honey
750-ml/26-fl. oz. bottle
  Prosecco, chilled
375 ml/1½ cups palm wine
ice cubes, to serve

muslin/cheesecloth, for straining
a 1-litre/4-cup capacity jug/
  pitcher

SERVES 6-8 FLY PEOPLE

PREPARE THE PAW PAW
Peel and deseed both paw paws, chop them into chunks and throw the flesh of 1 paw paw into a blender or food processor (reserving a few chunks to serve). Add the sugarcane syrup or honey and 150 ml/⅔ cup water and blend until smooth.

Strain the blended mixture through a muslin into a bowl.

GET MIXING
Add ice cubes to a large jug and pour in the blended and strained paw paw mixture.

Pour in the chilled Prosecco, followed by the palm wine and stir to combine. Add the reserved paw paw chunks and stir again.

Divide between serving glasses and serve.

SIT BACK, UNWIND & WATCH THE FACES OF YOUR GUESTS LIGHT UP AS THEY ENJOY

NAIJA JOY

When given a mood to choose we will always choose joy. There is nothing more satisfying than believing, manifesting your goals and achieving them. We all deserve joy and what better way to toast than with this vibrant green cocktail that pays homage to our motherland home.

150 ml/⅔ cup gold Tequila (we like Don Julio)
50 ml/scant ¼ cup fresh lime juice
180 ml/¾ cup blue Curaçao
180 ml/¾ cup pineapple juice
ice cubes, to shake

TO GARNISH
30 g/1 oz. Chin Chin biscuits/cookies (homemade, see page 128, or shop-bought), finely crushed
30 g/2 tablespoons brown sugar
1 lime wedge
3 pineapple wedges

SERVES 3 FLY PEOPLE

FIRST RIM THE GLASSES
Put the sugar and crushed chin chin on a plate. Use the lime wedge to rub around each glass rim and roll each one in the sugar and crumb mixture to coat with delicious sweet goodness. Set aside until needed.

GET MIXING!
Fill a cocktail shaker with ice cubes.

Pour in the tequila, lime juice, blue curaçao and pineapple juice.

SHAKE WHAT YOUR MAMA GAVE YOU!
Half fill each glass with ice cubes and divide the vibrant green mixture equally between them. Garnish with a pineapple wedge.

ENJOYMENT TODAY, TOMORROW AND THE NEXT DAY IS YOURS!

APPLE PIE MOJITO

We combined our mum's favourite drink with one of our family's favourite desserts.

4–6 fresh mint leaves
9 thin slices sweet eating apple
135 ml/½ cup Bacardi white rum
90 ml/⅓ cup Weston apple cider or apple juice
45 ml/3 tablespoons fresh lime juice
45 ml/3 tablespoons simple syrup
chilled club soda, to top up
ice cubes

TO RIM
1 lime wedge (to rub around the rim)
1 tablespoon ground sweet cinnamon
50 g/¼ cup white caster/superfine sugar

TO GARNISH
3 long cinnamon sticks
3 thin slices sweet eating apple (such as Pink Lady)

SERVES 3 FLY PEOPLE

FIRST, RIM THE GLASSES
Mix the ground cinnamon with the sugar on a plate. Grab 3 highball glasses, use the lime wedge to rub around the rim and roll the rim of the glass into the mixture all the way round so it rims the glass with cinnamon sugar.

In a cocktail shaker, crush the fresh mint leaves and apple slices gently to release their flavours. Fill the shaker with ice cubes and then add the rum, apple cider or apple juice, lime juice and simple syrup.

PLAY 'ISKABA' BY WANDE COAL AND SHAKE IT LIKE YOUR LIFE DEPENDS ON IT!
Shake until chilled and all those wonderful flavours combine.

Add ice cubes to the rimmed glasses and fill each one with one-third of the mixture in the strainer.

Top up with club soda. Add a cinnamon stick as a stirrer and an apple slice to the rim of each glass.

ENJOY THE PARTY IN YOUR MOUTH!

UNCLE'S SANGARIA

It is no secret that the Nigerian uncles love whisky. You will catch them at every African motive swearing to just have one and laughing with fellow uncles they haven't caught up with in a while. Once they have added a cheeky whisky on the rocks, expect words of wisdom and African proverbs to fill your ears. We created this banger inspired by our Dad and uncles in their thousands who love a good time. Even if you're not a whisky lover, this one will have you perched in the corner resisting your Dad's.

450 ml/½ bottle of white wine (Sancerre white wine is our fave, but you can use any)
240 ml/1 cup whisky (Chivas Regal – it's our Dad's favourite)
100 ml/scant ½ cup triple sec or Cointreau
300 ml/1¼ cups non-alcoholic grape wine
120 ml/½ cup freshly squeezed lemon juice
2 tablespoons granulated sugar (adjust to taste)
300 g/10½ oz. white grapes, cut in half
1 lemon, thinly sliced
2 limes, thinly sliced
1 apple, cored and thinly sliced
100 g/⅔ cup mixed berries
ice cubes
240 ml/1 cup soda water or lemon-lime soda (optional, for serving)
100 g/2 cups fresh mint leaves

a large jug/pitcher

SERVES 4-6 FLY PEOPLE

START ADDING THE FLAVOUR

In a large jug, combine the white wine, whiskey, Cointreau, non-alcoholic grape wine, lemon juice and granulated sugar. Stir until the sugar is dissolved.

Add the grapes, lemon slices, lime slices, apple slices and mixed berries to the jug and stir gently to combine.

Cover the jug and refrigerate the sangria for at least 2–4 hours, or preferably overnight, to allow the flavours to meld together.

DON'T BE SHY, IF YOU WANT MORE SUGAR, ADD IT - ENJOYMENT IS GOOD FOR YOU!

Fill glasses with ice and top with Uncle's Sangria. If desired, top each glass with a splash of soda water or lemon-lime soda for added fizz.

Garnish each glass with fresh mint leaves, if desired.

SERVE FAST FAST

MAMI WATERMELON

'Mami water' is the goddess of water in Nigerian mythology, derived from pigeon English meaning 'mother of water'. When we were kids our mother told us stories of mermaids being spotted out at sea by fishermen and even swore she spotted one herself in the sea. We always loved this story and imagined a beautiful pink tail and imagined the sunlight as it reflected off her scales. We wanted to capture this in a cocktail and created this Flygerian masterpiece that's vibrant, warm and rich in colour like the mermaid we imagined as kids.

500 g/1 lb. 2 oz. fresh watermelon, the riper the better

400 ml/1⅔ cups gin (we love to use Hendrick's gin)

100 ml /scant ½ cup agave syrup

100 ml/scant ½ cup fresh lime juice

200 ml/scant 1 cup soda water, to top up

ice

RIM GARNISH

lime wedge

100 g/3½ oz. dried edible pink flowers, crushed

100 g/½ cup soft light brown sugar

4 wedges of watermelon

SERVES 4 FLY PEOPLE

RIM THE GLASSES
Place the crushed edible flowers and brown sugar on a flat plate and mix together well. Rim 4 highball glasses by running a lime wedge around the rim of the glasses, then dipping the rim into the flower and sugar mixture.

START BLENDING
Blend the watermelon with 100 ml/scant ½ cup water to make a purée.

Add ice to the glasses and ice to a cocktail shaker.

Add the gin, agave syrup, blended watermelon and lime juice.

SHAKE IT BABY, DON'T BREAK IT
Shake the cocktail mixer for 30 seconds.

GRAB YOUR SPEAKER & PLAY 'SOKE' BY BURNA BOY
Pour into the tall glasses and top each one with soda water.

Add a watermelon wedge to the side of the glass without the rim detail and enjoy!

INDEX

adegreg steak bake 48
agege bread 23
 agege bread & butter
  pudding 136
 Naija French toast 132
agoyin sauce: ewa agoyin
 30
akara 12
 akara bean fritters 29
amala 91
apples: Apple Pie Mojito
 169
 chin chin crumble 131
'arancini', jollof 47
asun turkey bites 117
ayamase stew 70

Bailey's: plantain & Bailey's
 ice cream 142
bake, adegreg steak 48
bananas: chin'offee pie 135
 Plantain Colada 164
banga soup 63
beans 17
 akara bean fritters 29
 ewa agoyin 30
 seafood okra soup 56
 steamed bean pudding 26
 vegan edikang gong 64
beef 16
 adegreg steak bake 48
 banga soup 63
 beef suya 36
 beef suya spring rolls 43
 egusi soup 59
 Naija plantain & slow-
  cooked tacos 109–10
 Nigerian 'meat' pies 108
 one-pot ogbono soup 60
berries: Uncle's Sangria 170
bitter leaves 15
 banga soup 63
black-eyed beans: akara
  bean fritters 29
 ewa agoyin 30
 steamed bean pudding 26
blue Curaçao: Naija Joy 169
blueberries: plantain souffle
 pancakes 120
bread: agege bread 23
 agege bread & butter
  pudding 136
 Naija French toast 132
buttery cassava mash 92

cabbage: Lekki express
 Nigerian shawarma 99
caramel: chin'offee pie 135

cashew nuts: sugarcane
 cash cookies 141
cassava 15
 buttery cassava mash 92
 twice-cooked cassava
  chips 100
cheese: jollof 'arancini' 47
 Naija plantain & slow-
  cooked tacos 109–10
 warm plantain, halloumi &
  walnut salad 84
cheesecake, Milo raspberry
 coolie 124
chicken 16
 Lekki express Nigerian
  shawarma 99
 mighty Supermalt wings
  37
 premium fried rice 55
chicken gizzards: gizdodo
 skewers 33
chillies/chiles: asun turkey
 bites 117
 ayamase stew 70
 beef suya 36
 chilli h'oil 19
 ewa agoyin 30
 Ghanian shito 20
 'Give it to Dem' Chilli
  Lychee Margarita 150
 one-pot peppered goat
  meat 74
 steamed bean pudding 26
chin chin biscuits 10, 128
 chin chin crumble 131
 chin'offee pie 135
 Lagos mess 136
 Milo raspberry coolie
  cheesecake 124
chips and fries: dodo chips
 103
 Naija fish 'n' chips 80
 okra fries 104
 plantain fries 12, 103
 twice-cooked cassava
  chips 100
chocolate: agege bread &
 butter pudding 136
cider: Apple Pie Mojito 169
coconut milk: Plantain
 Colada 164
condensed milk: chin'offee
 pie 135
 Naija Guinness punch 161
cookies, sugarcane 141
cooking methods 12
crayfish 16
 ayamase stew 70
 chilli h'oil 19
cream: chin'offee pie 135
 Lagos mess 136

Milo raspberry coolie
 cheesecake 124
Naija Guinness punch 161
plantain & Bailey's ice
 cream 142
cream cheese: Milo
 raspberry coolie
 cheesecake 124
croquettes, prawn 40
crumble, chin chin 131
cucumber: cucumber
 Margarita 149
 Zobo Dreams 154
curry powder: egusi soup 59
 roast lamb 81

dipping sauce, sweet bell
 pepper 103
don't be basic Indomie
 noodles 96
doughnuts, Nigerian 127
dried fruit: agege bread &
 butter pudding 136

eba 91
edikang gong, vegan 64
efo riro: vegan efo riro
 spinach stew 71
eggs: ayamase stew 70
 egg roll 113
 eggy Nigerian-style
  omelette 114
 Naija French toast 132
 plantain & Bailey's ice
  cream 142
 steamed bean pudding 26
egusi soup 59
evaporated milk: chin chin
 128
 Naija Guinness punch 161
ewa agoyin 30

fish 16
 Naija fish 'n' chips 80
 one-pot ogbono soup 60
 steamed bean pudding 26
Flygerian jollof rice 52
French toast, Naija 132
fries see chips and fries
fritters, akara bean 29
fufu, plantain 92

garlic 16
 jollof spaghetti 77
 oxtail stew 68
garri 17
 eba 91
gin: Mami Watermelon 173
ginger 16
 Ginger Me immune
  booster 164

'Give it to Dem' Chilli
 Lychee Margarita 150
gizdodo skewers 33
goat 16
 banga soup 63
 egusi soup 59
 one-pot ogbono soup 60
 one-pot peppered goat
  meat 74
grape wine: Uncle's Sangria
 170
grenadine syrup: Lagos rise
 & shine 157
Guinness 17
 Guinness pork ribs 44
 Naija Guinness punch 161

halloumi: plantain, halloumi
 & walnut salad 84
hibiscus (zobo) leaves:
 Zobo Dreams 154
honey: plantain, halloumi &
 walnut salad 84

ice cream, plantain &
 Bailey's 142
Indomie noodles, don't be
 basic 96
ingredients 15–17

jollof: Flygerian jollof rice 52
 jollof 'arancini' 47
 jollof spaghetti 77

kale: vegan edikang gong 64
Kiwi Strawberry Crush 149

Lagos mess 136
Lagos rise & shine 157
lamb: roast lamb Flygerian
 style 81
Lekki express Nigerian
 shawarma 99
lemon juice: Mr Chaps 146
 Party No De Stop Cocktail
  158
lime juice: cucumber
 Margarita 149
 Kiwi Strawberry Crush 149
 Plantain Colada 164
locust beans 17
 seafood okra soup 56
 vegan edikang gong 64
lychee juice: 'Give it to Dem'
 Chilli Lychee Margarita
 150

Mami Watermelon 173
mangetout/snow peas:
 don't be basic Indomie
 noodles 96

Margaritas: cucumber
Margarita 149
'Give it to Dem' Chilli
Lychee Margarita 150
Martini, Supermalt 157
meats 16
ayamase stew 70
banga soup 63
egusi soup 59
one-pot ogbono soup 60
see also chicken; lamb, etc
meringue: Lagos mess 136
mighty Supermalt wings 37
Milo powder: chin'offee pie
135
Milo raspberry coolie
cheesecake 124
Mr Chaps 146
moi moi 26

Naija fish 'n' chips 80
Naija French toast 132
Naija Guinness punch 161
Naija Joy 169
Naija plantain & slow-
cooked tacos 109–10
Nigerian 'meat' pies 108
Nigerian doughnuts 127
noodles, don't be basic
Indomie 96

ofada rice 88
ogbono: one-pot ogbono
soup 60
okra 15
okra fries 104
seafood okra soup 56
omelette, eggy Nigerian-
style 114
one-pot ogbono soup 60
one-pot peppered goat
meat 74
orange juice: Lagos rise &
shine 157
Mr Chaps 146
Zobo Dreams 154
oxtail stew 68

palm wine, paw paw 165
pancakes, plantain souffle
120
Party No De Stop Cocktail
158
pasta: jollof spaghetti 77
paw paw palm wine 165
peanut oil: chilli h'oil 19
peanuts: beef suya 36
beef suya spring rolls 43
sugarcane cookies 141
peppers 15
adegreg steak bake 48

asun turkey bites 117
ayamase stew 70
beef suya spring rolls 43
gizdodo skewers 33
jollof spaghetti 77
Naija fish 'n' chips 80
Naija plantain & slow-
cooked tacos 109–10
one-pot peppered goat
meat 74
peppered prawns 67
roast lamb 81
steamed bean pudding 26
sweet bell pepper dipping
sauce 103
pies: chin'offee pie 135
Nigerian 'meat' pies 108
pineapple: Ginger Me
immune booster 164
pineapple juice: Naija Joy
169
Plantain Colada 164
Zobo Dreams 154
plantain 15
gizdodo skewers 33
Naija plantain & slow-
cooked tacos 109–10
plantain & Bailey's ice
cream 142
plantain chips 12
Plantain Colada 164
plantain fries/dodo chips
103
plantain fufu 92
plantain souffle pancakes
120
plantain waffles 123
warm plantain, halloumi &
walnut salad 84
pork ribs, Guinness 44
prawns/shrimp: ayamase
stew 70
don't be basic Indomie
noodles 96
peppered prawns 67
prawn croquettes 40
premium fried rice 55
steamed bean pudding 26
Prosecco: paw paw palm
wine 165
puff pastry: adegreg steak
bake 48
puff puff 10, 127
punch, Naija Guinness 161

raspberries: Milo raspberry
coolie cheesecake 124
rice: Flygerian jollof rice 52
jollof 'arancini' 47
ofada rice 88
premium fried rice 55

rum: Apple Pie Mojito 169
Kiwi Strawberry Crush 149
Naija Guinness Punch 161
Plantain Colada 164

salad, warm plantain,
halloumi & walnut 84
seafood okra soup 56
shawarma, Lekki express
Nigerian 99
shiitake mushrooms: vegan
edikang gong 64
shito, Ghanian 20
skewers: beef suya 36
gizdodo skewers 33
souffle pancakes, plantain
120
soups 12
banga soup 63
egusi soup 59
one-pot ogbono soup 60
seafood okra soup 56
spaghetti, jollof 77
speculoos: Naija French
toast 132
spinach: edikang gong 64
efo riro spinach stew 71
eggy Nigerian-style
omelette 114
egusi soup 59
one-pot ogbono soup 60
spring rolls, beef suya 43
stews 12
ayamase stew 70
efo riro spinach stew 71
oxtail stew 68
stockfish 17
ayamase stew 70
banga soup 63
strawberries: Kiwi
Strawberry Crush 149
Lagos mess 136
plantain souffle pancakes
120
sugarcane cookies 141
Supermalt: mighty
Supermalt wings 37
Supermalt Martini 157
suya 10, 12
beef suya 36
beef suya spring rolls 43
sweet bell pepper dipping
sauce 103

tacos, Naija plantain &
slow-cooked 109–10
tequila: Cucumber
Margarita 149
'Give it to Dem' Chilli
Lychee Margarita 150
Lagos Rise & Shine 157

Naija Joy 169
Party No De Stop Cocktail
158
tofu: vegan edikang gong 64
tomatoes 15
adegreg steak bake 48
beef suya 36
efo riro spinach stew 71
egusi soup 59
ewa agoyin 30
Flygerian jollof rice 52
gizdodo skewers 33
jollof spaghetti 77
Naija plantain & slow-
cooked tacos 109–10
oxtail stew 68
roast lamb 81
sweet bell pepper dipping
sauce 103
tortilla wraps: Lekki express
Nigerian shawarma 99
triple sec: Cucumber
Margarita 149
'Give it to Dem' Chilli
Lychee Margarita 150
Party No De Stop Cocktail
158
Uncle's Sangria 170
turkey: asun turkey bites
117

Uncle's Sangria 170

vegan akara bean fritters 29
vegan edikang gong 64
vegan efo riro spinach stew
71
vegetables: premium fried
rice 55
vermouth: Supermalt
Martini 157
vodka: Mr Chaps 146
Supermalt Martini 157
Zobo Dreams 154

waffles, plantain 123
walnuts: plantain, halloumi
& walnut salad 84
watermelon: Mami
Watermelon 173
whiskey: Uncle's Sangria
170
wine: Uncle's Sangria 170

yams 15
pounded yam 88

Zobo 12
Zobo Dreams 154

ACKNOWLEDGEMENTS

We want to thank those who gave us life, shaped our upbringing and made this book possible.

Our sensational parents:
Gloria Shomope-Edun
Godspower Christopher Edun

Our beautiful siblings:
Samuel, Christopher, David, Florence, James Joshua and Josephine Faith Edun

To all of our cousins, aunties and uncles in London, Nigeria and across the world.

Our incredible Flygerian team.

The Peckham Palms Team for their amazing support.

Seamstress and hairdresser Adigo Abimaje – aka Tessy – for our outfits featured and unshakable support (Instagram @dbqlabel and @de_black_qrown).

Thank you to Pete Rossi for the logo and branding, and always championing us! Legend.

All our friends in the 'Ravey Days' Whatsapp group for always believing in us and speaking our name into rooms we are yet to enter.

K and A butchers on Peckham High street for our 10/10 supplies weekly.

Everyone that helped us on this beautiful journey to create this book:
Shoot team: Clare Winfield, Kathy Kordalis and Max Robinson, Sadie Albuquerque, Grace Jenkins and Arnaud Berrabia
RPS team: Julia Charles, Abi Waters, Leslie Harrington, Megan Smith, Patricia Harrington, Yvonne Doolan and Jack Duce.

Nick Dear: PR manager.

In loving memory of
(clockwise from left)

Gbenga Michael Adegbite

Oluwabukola Ajayi

Our Grandma
Mary Uhunamure
Obahiagbon

Uncle Frank